T0345884

Linear Thought - Condensation

Peter Magyar

ORO
EDITIONS

Table of Contents

Introduction

They still can be beautiful, but pararmetric algorithms do not have souls. Humans do. Therefore, in architecural design, we have to unify knowing and feeling. This unification can only happen through the physical and cognitive act of drawing. We have to exhaust as many potentials as possible to arrive to a condensed entitiy, which latently contains the essences of several previously unverbalaized thougths.

Architecural design is, even in its embryonic stage, a thought-condensing process. We cannot know these thoughts, but certainly we can feel them. From the intensity of the "heat"—our passion—during the distillation phase, to the patience and the precision of this translating act—from spirit to matter—designs might acquire the most coveted quality – timelessness.

Earlier attempts to explain this process failed, but I have created a pair of words, which make it easy to remember the process described above:

Plot: among its less common meanings can refer to plan, design, dream up, and construct.
Clot: referring to concentration or coagulation into something acceptable.

So I christened these thought-condensation products "plotclots." I have quite a few of them; some were constructed while others are just contemplated, or even interrupted in different phases the conceiving act. All are drawn—with more or less details and precision—with ink on paper; the original physical traces of the otherwise ephemeral, intangible thought.

In *Linear Thought-condensation* I have collected seven of these plotclot processes. As in my earlier books I implore the reader to read the drawings. Always interested in the process, moreso than in the product, I dare to state that there are very few, if any, other collections where one can "read" the mind of an architect. Of course, being a romantic, I am still more interested in the heart, which has more common qualities with our fellow humans.

Many times I am puzzled by the perceived one-sidedness of architects who talk about space and drawing nonspace. Decades ago, to allow for the simultaneous drawing and viewing of space and nonspace "spaceprints" were employed, which, as surfaces, fully represented both domains. With their invention and articulation, real circumstantial-singularities can be created, which are in my—in this case not so humble—opinion way beyond the products of mere problem-soliving methods.

Foreword - György Szegő

An architect, to some extent, always has to deal with applied science. I view the drawings of Peter Magyar as fundamental research. Digital presentation today is unquestionably part of an architect's work. We do not yet know how this will change architects' points of view and methods in terms of their creativity and their approach to projects. Since Vitruvius we have considered drawings as the conception of a building preceding its birth. The relationship between drawing and constructed buildings, also explored by painters, has changed in the last two to three thousand years exactly in that particular border area which Peter Magyar focuses on in his work and exhibitions.

More specifically, he shows how the unknown is transformed in the field of the preconscious where he aspires to excavate reality from the unconscious using his stlye/stylus and his pen as a tool. This is creative work for him, the floating phase, which he would like to prolong as much as possible. The method consists of creating process drawings and he holds himself back from proceeding from the unknown to the known, as the routine of what is known, as many of us are aware, boring. I believe the state of uncertainty is a state of grace at a secret place of inspiration; an Icarian flight, as Peter Magyar puts it. But Peter Magyar, modestly, does not talk about this, even though his style is worthy of high literature. He prefers the act of flying.

His signature is embodied by his thousands of process drawings made with his fountain pen, which are the reflections of his architectural thoughts. It's exhilarating to see how the tactile becomes part of the perception in his work and how the lines created represent at the same time the thought and the spatial/material possibility of a later physical realisation. This is micro- and macro-cosmos at the same time.

The finger symbolically shown by Michelangelo in the Sistine Chapel as the magic wand of creation is in his case prolonged into a pen. (Peter is working on a sacral book entitled Spatial Fable for students of architecture, or even children, where he would address the readers of his tale in the following way: "and he began to write the next drawing. … He discovered the world outside, but even more, the secrets of his soul.")

Watching him draw, in the act of creation, one can see how disciplined he is: his pen is stopped because the gesture preceded the thought by the fraction of a second. Peter Magyar draws with a hyper perspective aimed at totality, and during this process he always has the vision of descriptive geometry under control – these experiences of foreground and background that are incidental and yet impossible to overwrite. This can be rarely reconciled with "one line drawing" technique but Peter Magyar always manages it. It should be mentioned that by doing so he preceded the appearance of this capability of computers. But it's more than a masterstroke: he draws new dimensions in an age when drawing has become automatic, an activity carried out by robots. This capability makes the oeuvre of Peter Magyar invaluable.

In our civilization we have only a few major changes of perspective, aimed at grasping reality. I am not talking about optics but perception, an activity that must be processed by nerve connections and the brain. The first milestone was the linear perspective uncovered in Pompeii. The second one the axonometric architectural drawing as seen on the paintings of Giotto that exceed the linear perspective. We attribute the perspectival picture of space projected onto a surface by precise drafting methods to Filippo Brunelleschi. The magicbox— similar to a camera obscura—used by Renaissance painters and drawers was also employed by Dürer to achieve precision for architectural environments (e.g. Saint Jerome). When drafting, it is the view of reality that is at stake, a view of perspective, defined by Alberti as a "window." Peter Magyar always makes this window appear.

Panofsky says that the "bursting" of the picture through the external plan towards the beholder and the penetration of the depicted space into the beholder's space (e.g., Van Eyck: Madonna in the Church, Crivelli: The Annunciation) are major turning points in our civilization. The topology of space neurons developed by Peter Magyar, a picture writer, via his drawing method, is also a turning point on a par with the above. They are represented at this exhibition by the "Palladian space neurons" drawings. Peter Magyar, who is incessantly writing the "details" of his spaceprint method into thousands of drawings may well be a milestone just like the above examples. He is a defining benchmark in an age marked by the progress of artificial intelligence.

The synergistic intelligence of vision and hand practiced by Peter Magyar is a promising human feedback of a mechanistic vision. It is an honor for the Budapest Kunsthalle to exhibit his work; I trust we are thereby "picture writing" history.

This essay is used with the permission of Dr. Szegő and is a reprint of his introduction for Peter Magyar's "Roots of Infinity" exhibition in the Kunsthalle of Budapest (October 2017).

Leon Battista Alberti: De pictura, 1435. Translated by Hajnóczi Gábor, Balassi Kiadó, Budapest, 1997.
Erwin Panofsky: A jelentés a vizuális művészetekben, Gondolat Kiadó, Budapest, 1984.

Brick-built God's House

Sanctuary and community center—overlapping but divided—was the main aspect of this church competition in Copenhagen, Denmark. Two unfinished sequences investigated how solemnity and simplicity can reinforce each other. The presence of water and the open plaza besides the building were the major entities, lending the otherwise very sober building an expected halo.

A staircase, leading up to the sightseeing roof-terrace stands for the almost obvious expression of ascendance in the first version. The simultaneous receptor of solar energy and the gesture of reaching for God's blessing was also an intended duality in the design.

The two functional domains—sacred and profane—are horizontally paired in the first version, while in the second they are above each other. This latter one—an addition to the tall and narrow sanctuary space—has a minimalistic bell tower, a symbol of the building type.

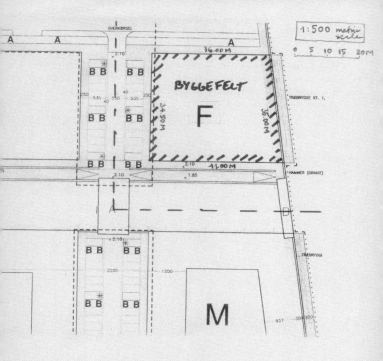

BYGGEFELT

F

M

1:500 metric scale

0 5 10 15 20M

OVERKØRSEL

36.00 M

34.50 M

11.00 M

TRÆBRYGGE KT. 1.

36.00 M

HAMMER (GRANIT)

TRÆBRYGGI

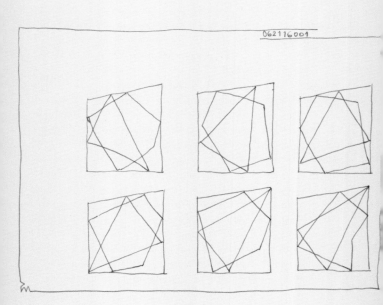

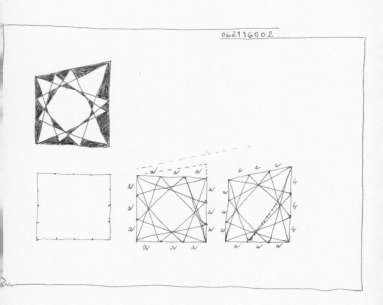

062116003/07
07

N

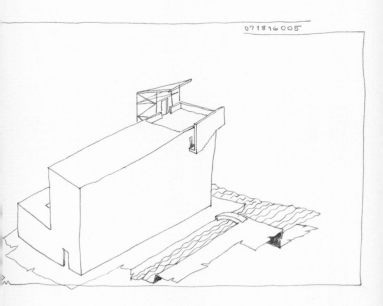

13

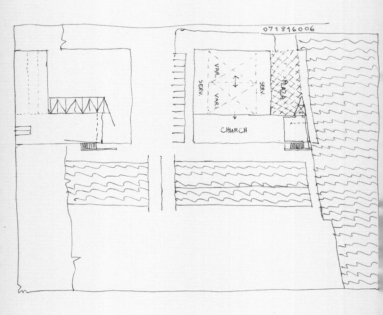

071816006

CHURCH

14

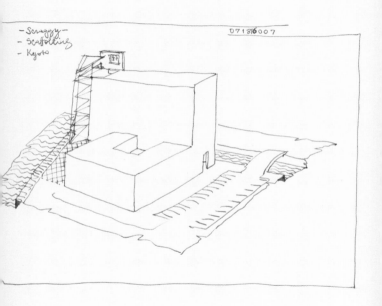

- Scraggy
- Scaffolding
- Kyoto

071816007

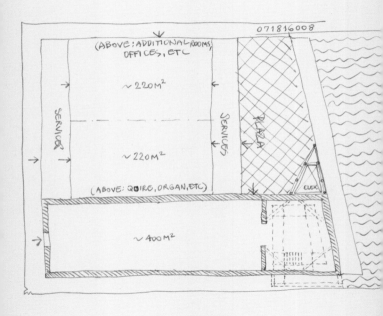

071816008

(ABOVE: ADDITIONAL ROOMS, OFFICES, ETC)

~220M²

SERVICES

SERVICES

PLAZA

~220M²

(ABOVE: QUIRE, ORGAN, ETC)

ELEV.

~400M²

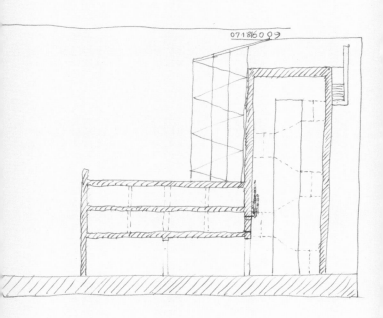

07 18 60 09

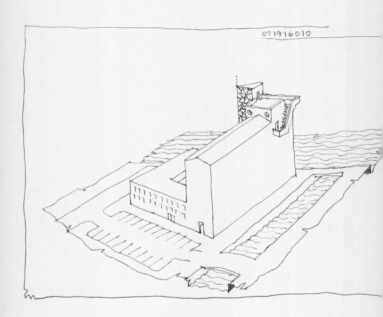

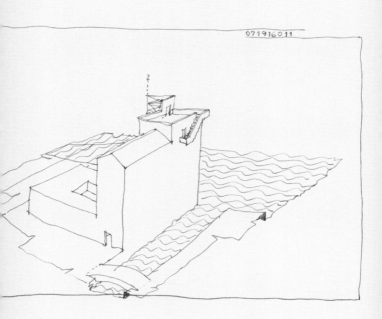

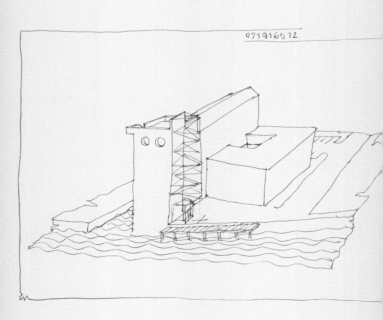

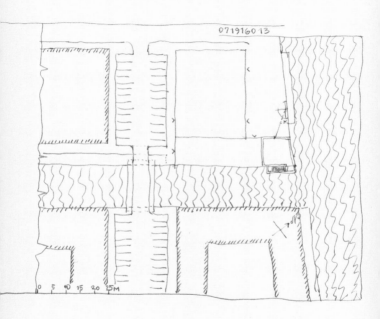

071916013

0 5 10 15 20 25M

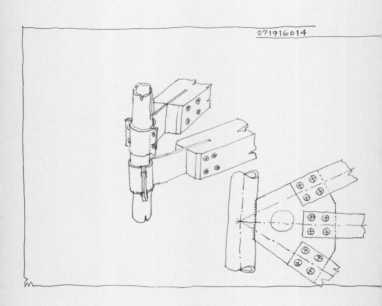

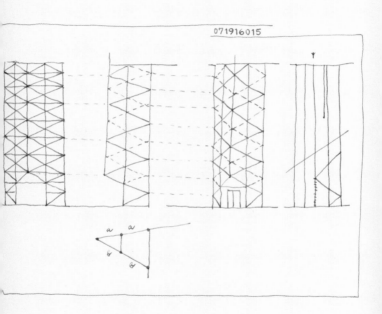

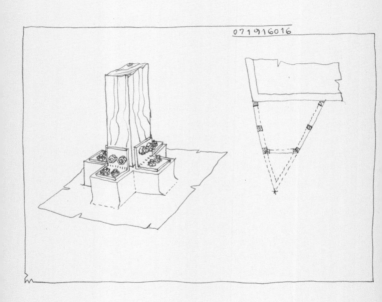

24

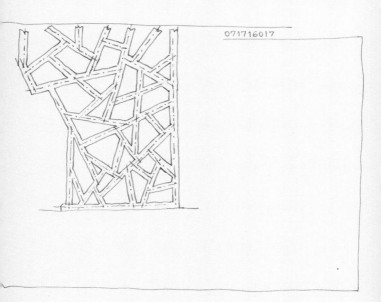

071716017

25

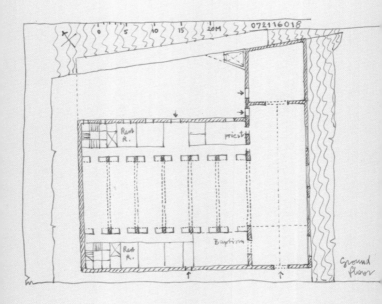

072116018

0 5 10 15 20M

Rest R.

priest

Baptism

Rest R.

Ground Floor

26

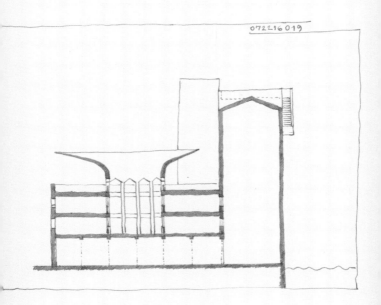

27

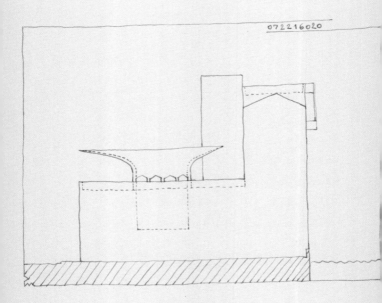

28

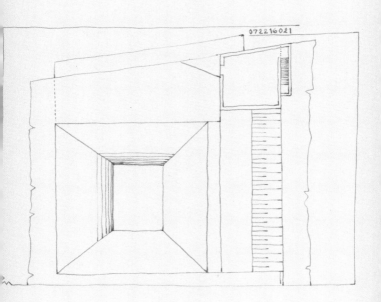

072216021

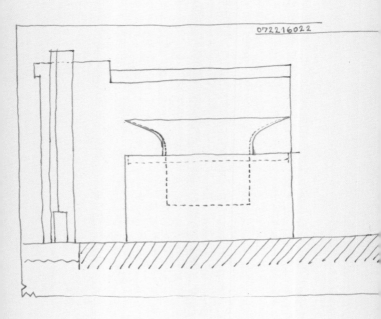

072216022

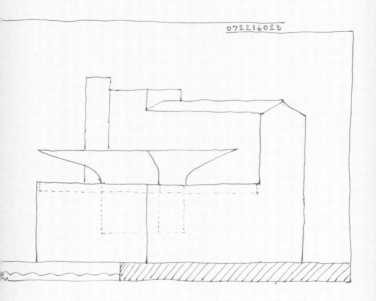

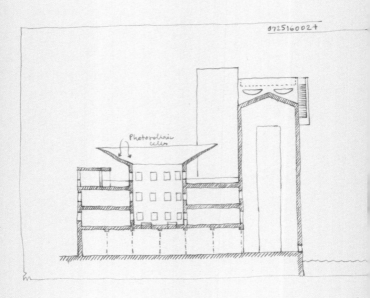

Photovoltaic cells

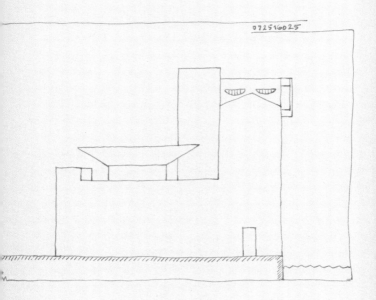

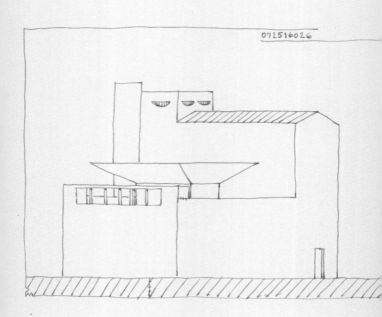

072516026

34

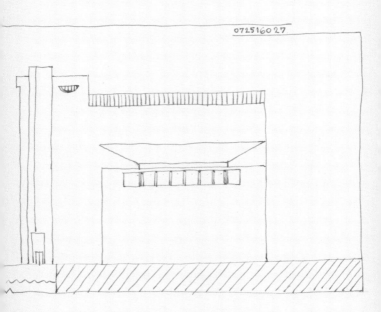

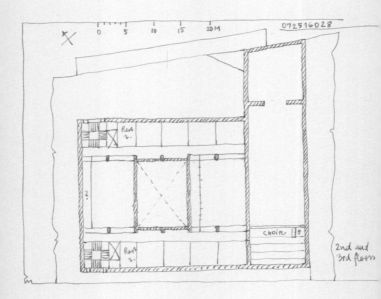

072516028

2nd and 3rd floors

36

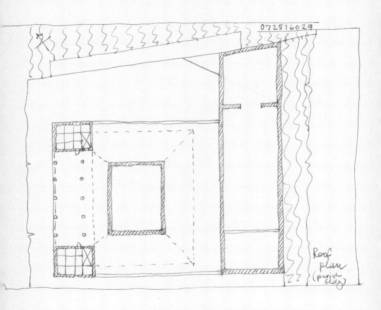

072516029

Roof
plan
(parish
bldg)

37

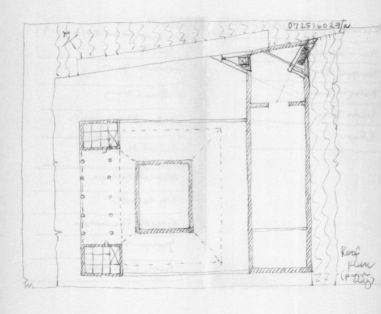

072516029/2

Roof
plan
(partial)

38

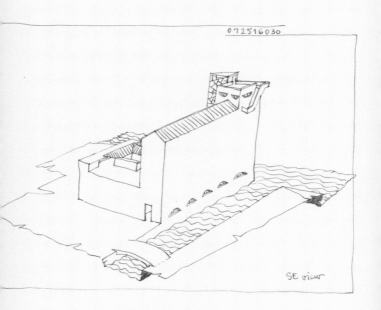

SE view

39

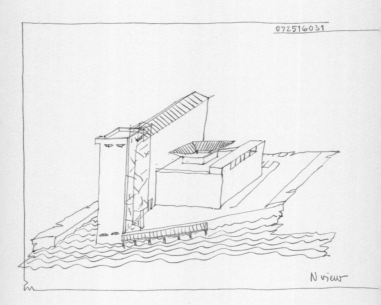

N view

40

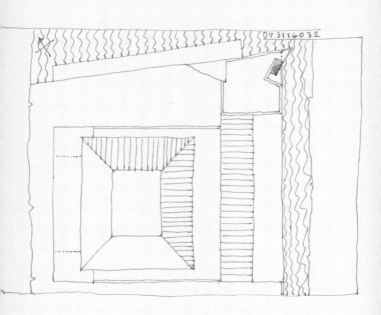

073116032

41

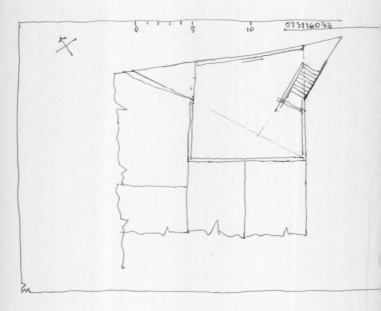

073116033

42

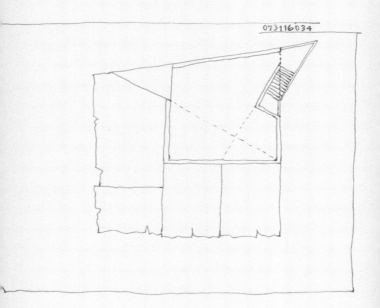

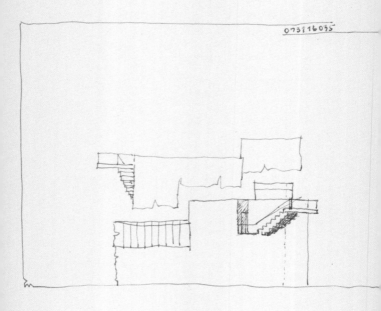

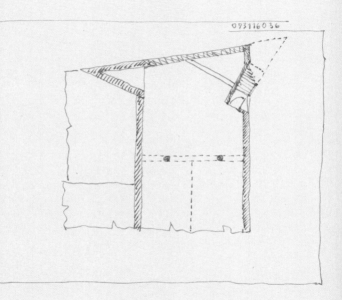

073116036

45

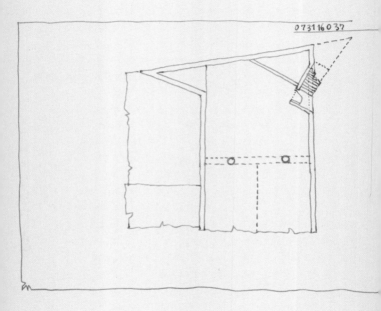

073116037

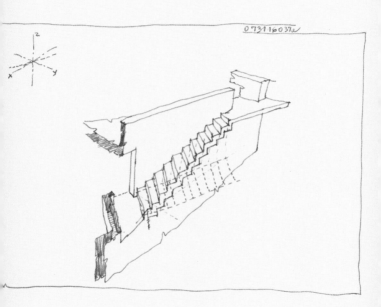

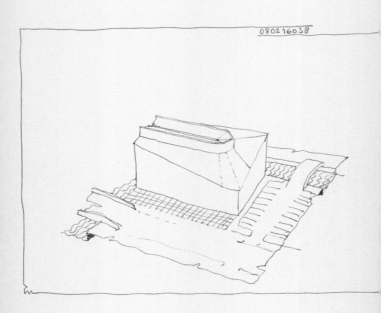

48

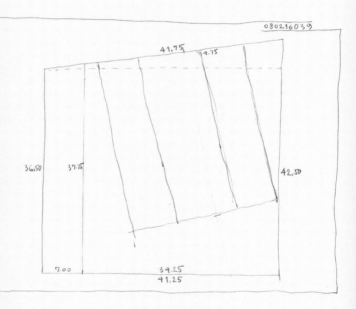

080216039

41.75   34.75

36.50   37.75   42.50

7.00   34.25

41.25

49

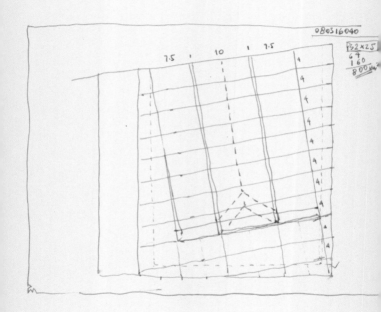

080316040

132×25
64
160
800 m²

7.5 | 10 | 7.5

4
4
4
4
4
4
41
4
4

50

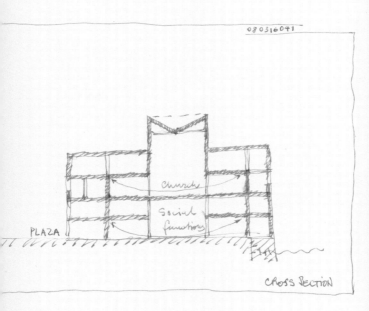

PLAZA

Church

Social functions

CROSS SECTION

51

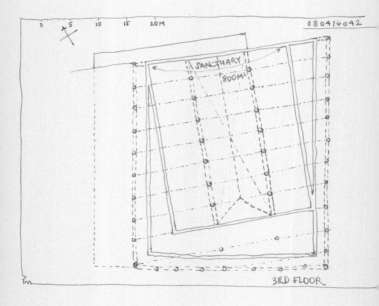

0   5   10   15   20M

080416042

SANCTUARY
800M²

3RD FLOOR

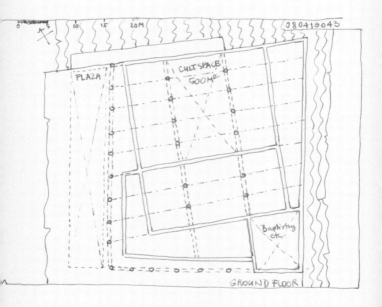

0 5 10 15 20M

080410043

PLAZA

CHLT SPACE
500M²

Baptistry
etc.

GROUND FLOOR

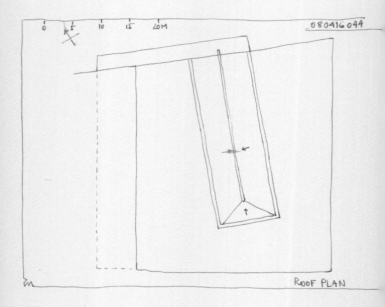

0 5 10 15 20M

ROOF PLAN

54

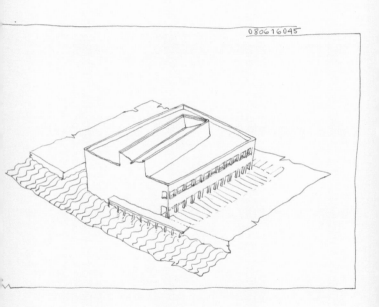

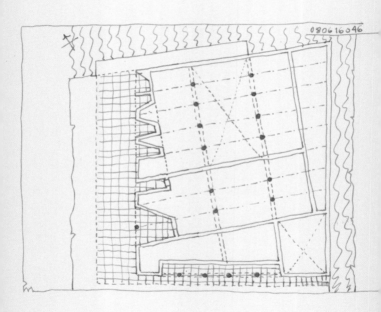

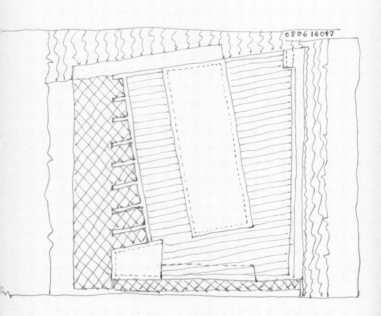

080616047

57

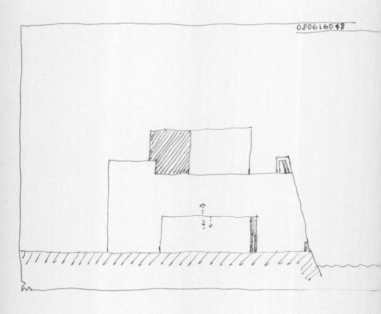

58

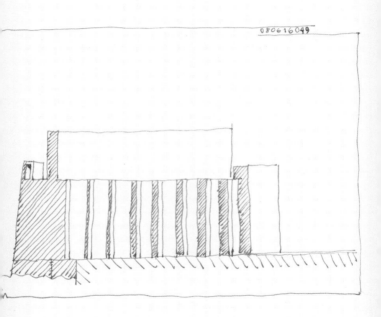

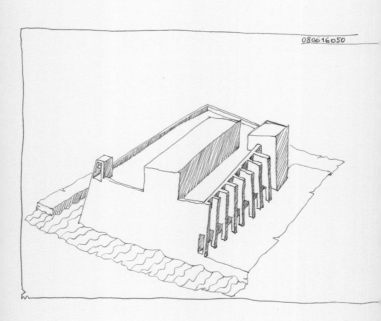

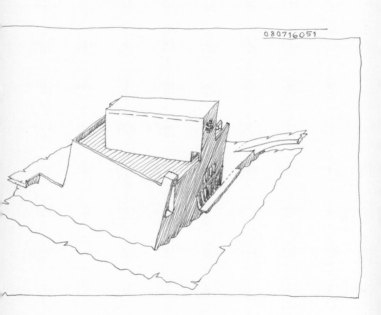

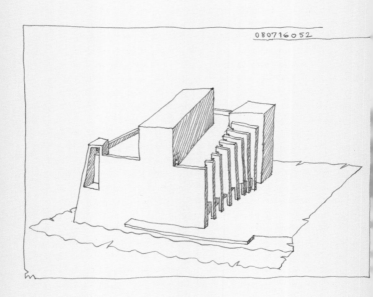

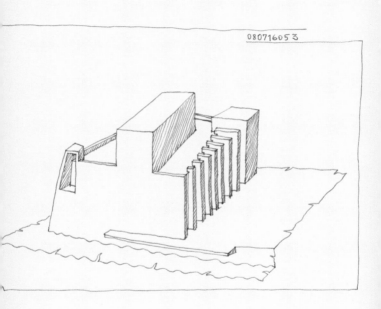

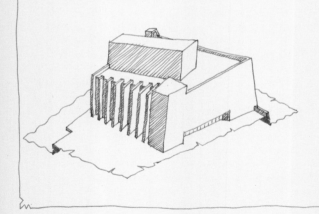

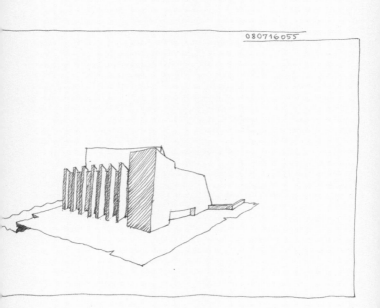

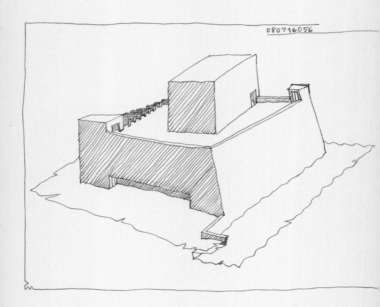

080716056

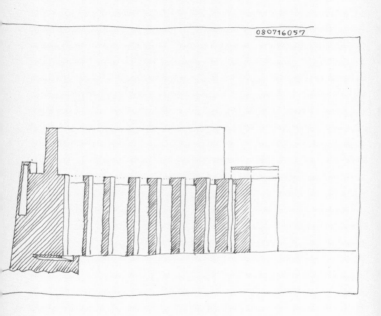

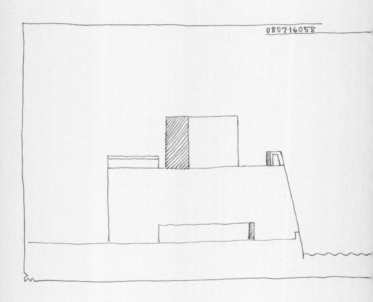

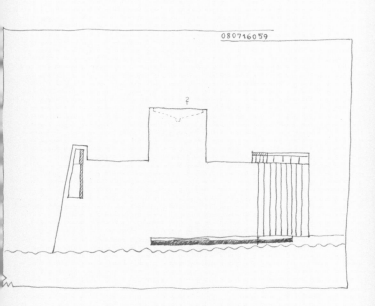

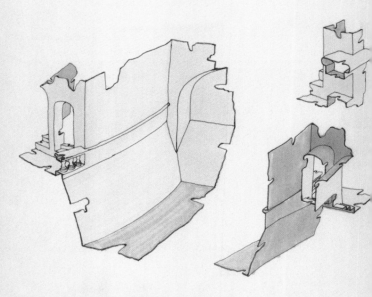

14. Spaceprints – Chateau Chambord. 1981

Schinkel Palace

The systemic interdependence of the parts to the whole is intensely investigated with this unfinished competition project. The late James Stirling was the one-person jury and requested a proposal for the great German architect's palace, as he would be alive today. A walled lot of 100 by 100 meters should contain the building, a secret garden, a little forest, and a small creek, among other elements.

The dignity of arrival, the ambiguity of the sunken garden and the first floor, which is on ground level, but becomes the piano nobile from the garden side, are among the first aspects explored by the drawings. Later, the "garden of the forking paths" provided the ring of choices, while in the middle, in the grand hall, rotated cubical intersections suggested to select between perceptional choices. The words in quotation marks are conceived independently from, but are identical with, the title of a poem by Garcia Lorca.

The multitude of the possible options, touched upon with the feast of a visual menu, offered many "paths" to follow with the design. Two of these were explored with focused attention.

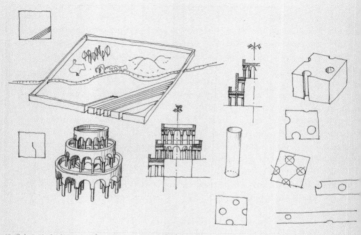

17 Schinkel House first variant 1979

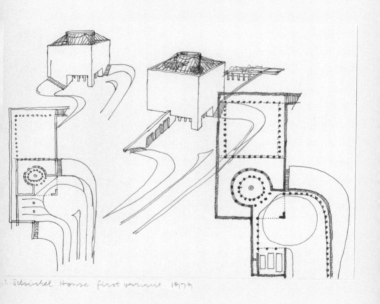

3. Schinkel House first variant 1979

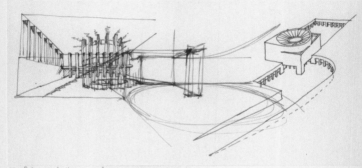

23. Schinkel House first version 1979

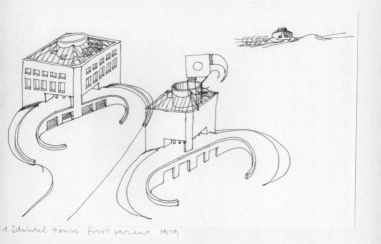

1. Schinkel House first variant 1979

75

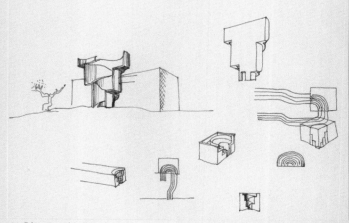

31. Schinkel House first variant 1979

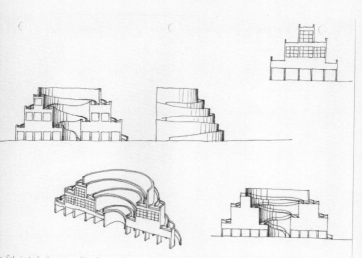

Schinkel House first version 1979

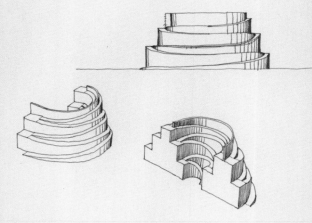

36. Schinkel House first variant 1979

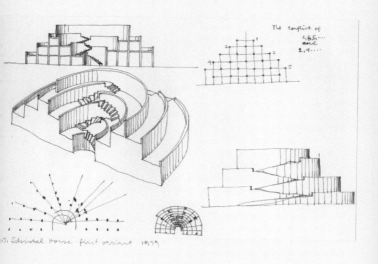

The conflict of
1,3,5....
and
2,4....

Schinkel House first variant 1979

79

38. Schinkel House first variant 1979

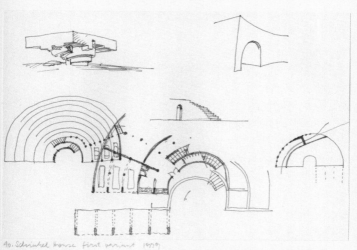

40. Schinkel House first variant 1979

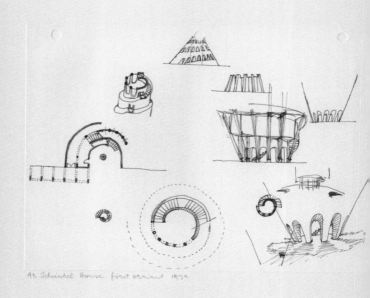

At Schinkel House first variant 1979

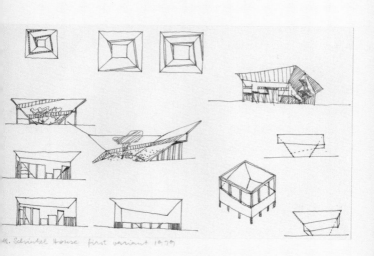

th. Schinkel House first variant 1979

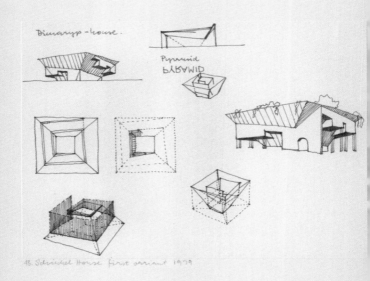

Dimayp - house.

Pyramid
PYRAMID

43. Schinkel House first variant 1979

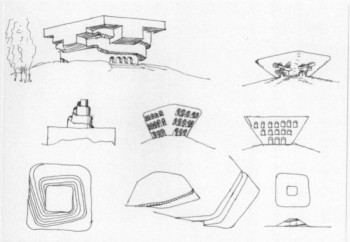

46. Schinkel House first variant 1979

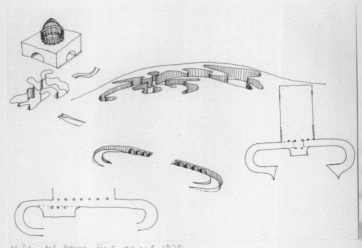

18. Schinkel House first variant 1979

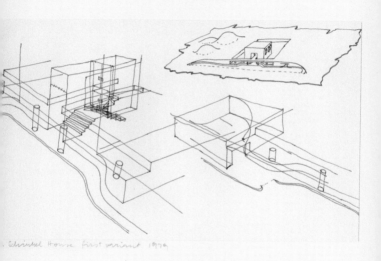

Schinkel House first variant 1979

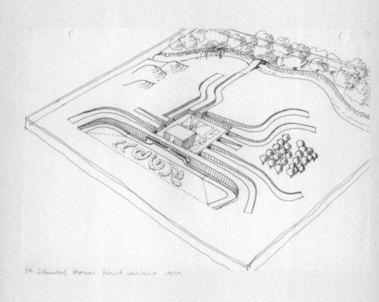

54. Schindel House first variant 1979

88

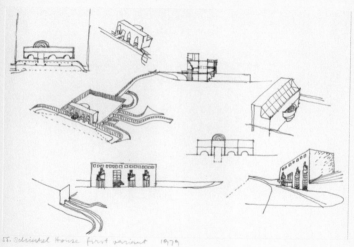

55. Schinkel House first variant 1979

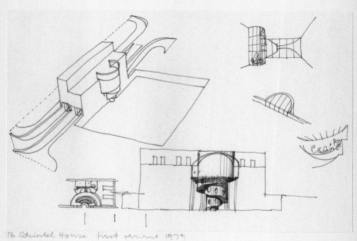

56 Schinkel House   first variant 1979

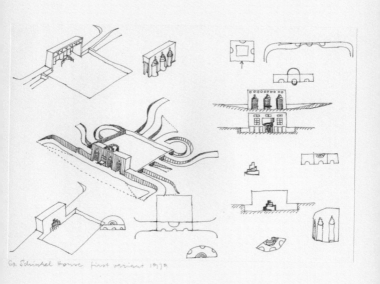

Schinkel House first project 1979

A. Schinkel House first variant 1979

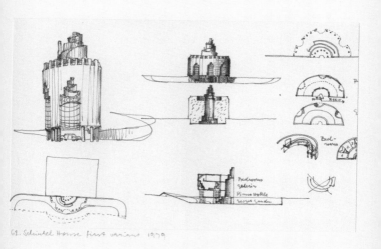

61. Schindel House first variant 1979

Pedraglio
galleria
Piano nobile
Secret garden

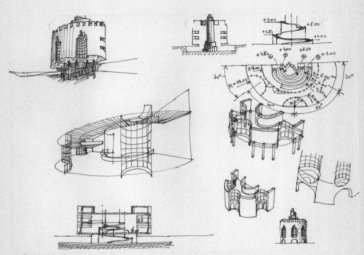

63. Schindel House first version 1979

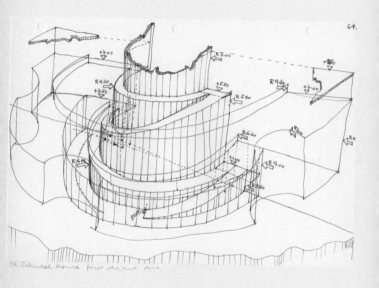

64. Schinkel House first variant 1974

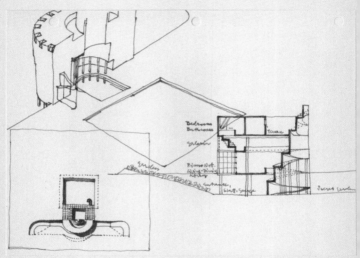

Bedrooms
Bathrooms

gallery

Terrace

Eridion

Piano Nob.
Living-Dining
lobby

entrance,
Serv. Space

Secret Garden

68. Schinkel House first variant 1979

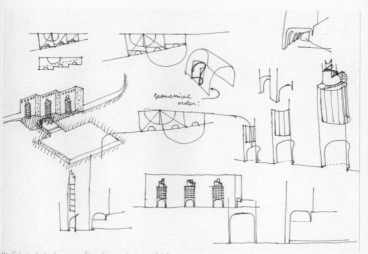

geometrical order!

70. Schinkel House first variant 1979

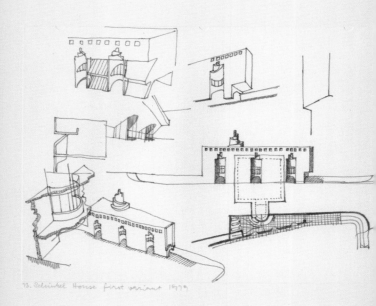

73. Schinkel House first variant 1979

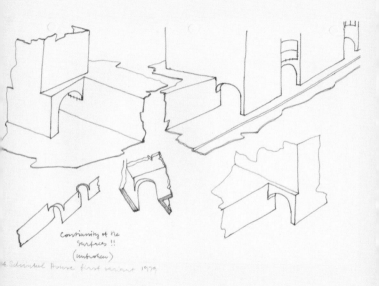

Continuity of the
surfaces !!
(unbroken)

4. Schinkel House first version 1979

99

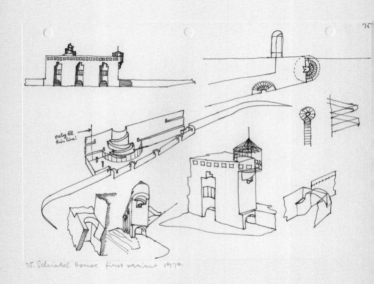

75. Schinkel House first variant 1978

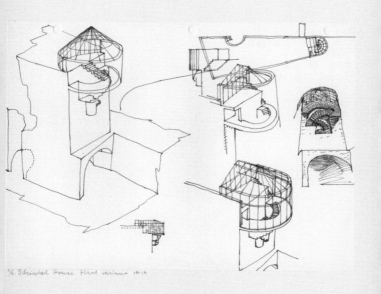

76. Schinkel House First variant 1979

101

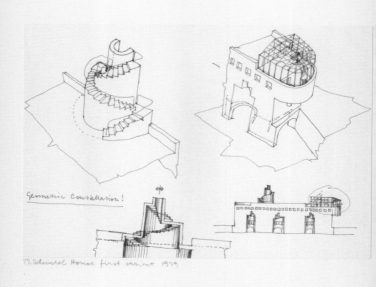

Geometric Constellation!

M. Schinkel House first variant 1979

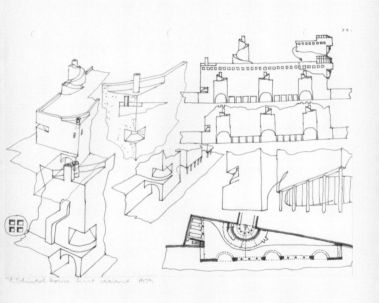

"8 Schindel House front variant 1974

103

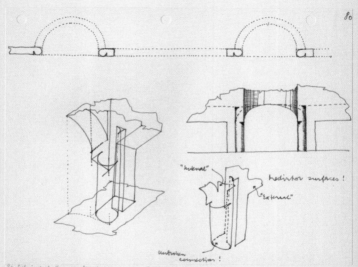

"internal"

radiator surfaces!

"external"

unbroken connection!

80. Schinkel House first variant 1979

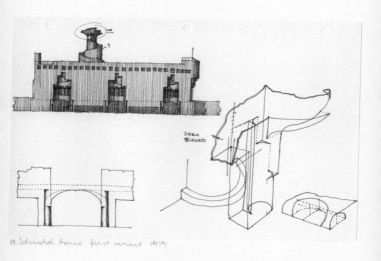

ZERO
THICKNESS

89. Schinkel House first variant 1979

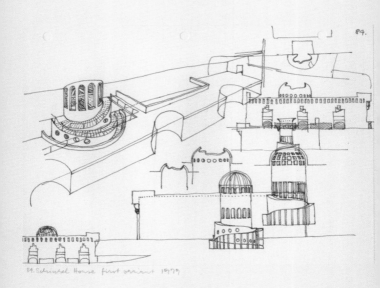

84. Schminkel House first variant 1979

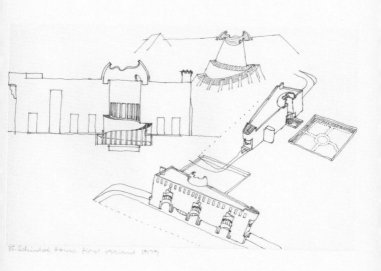

Schinkel House first variant 1979

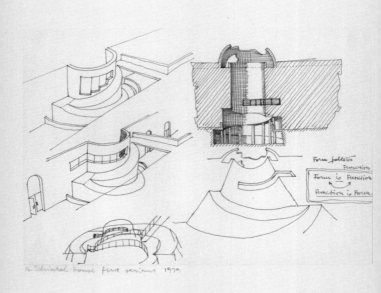

16. Schinkel house first version 1979

Form follows
Function

Form is Function

Function is Form.

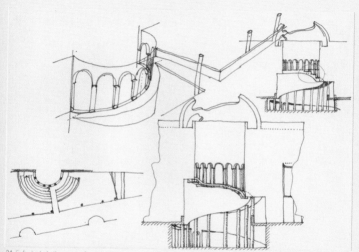

91. Schinkel House first variant 1970.

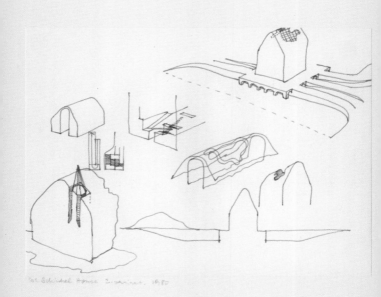

For Schindel House Drawings. 1980

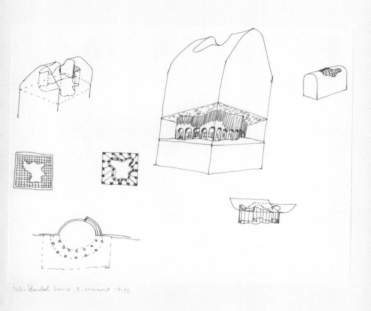

1935. Besichel house, 2. version 1k.50

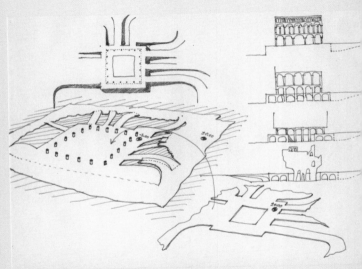

116. Schinkel Rome - Sud servant 1480

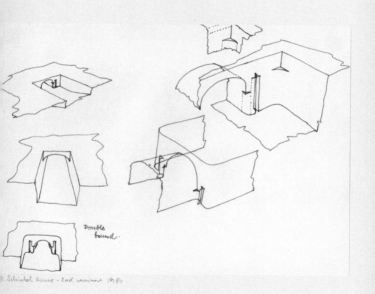

Double
bound.

Schinkel House – 2nd version 1980

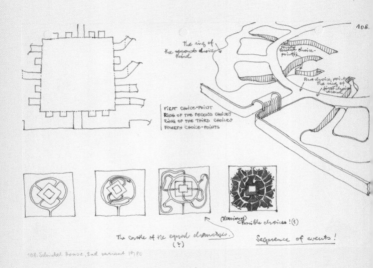

The ring of
the second choices
third

First choice points
The ring of
first choice second

FIRST CHOICE-POINT
RING OF THE SECOND CHOICES
RING OF THE THIRD CHOICES
FOURTH CHOICE-POINTS

108.

limited choice-points

(choosing)
possible choices! (?)

The circle of the equal chances.
(?)

Sequence of events!

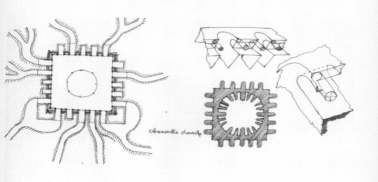

Observable chards

1114 Colonial house. Red variant 1980

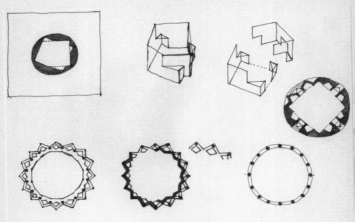

Introduction - Selection - Variation

113. Schindel House 2nd variant 1980

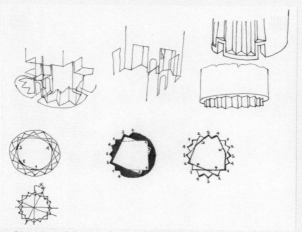

114. Schinkel house 2nd variant 19.80

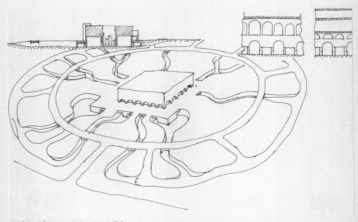

115. Schindel House 2nd version 1980

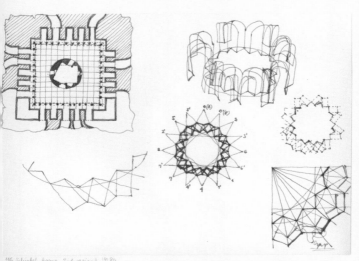

116. Schinkel House 2nd variant 1980

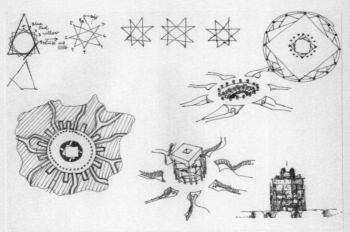

199. Schindel House 2nd variant 1980

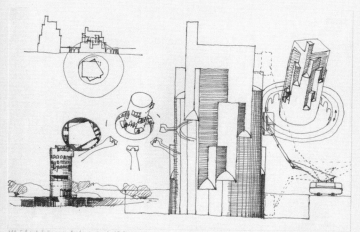

118. Schindel House. 2nd variant 1980

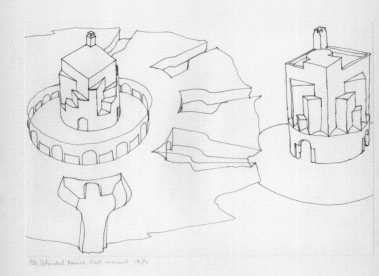

Re. Schindel House 2nd variant 19.80

Sixteen (8) Aspects of one possible (?) Reality (?)

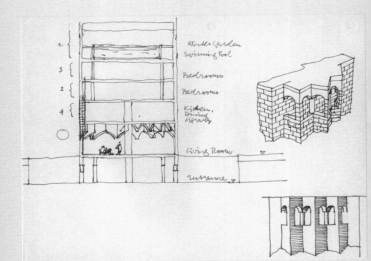

1. { } Winter Garden
Swimming Pool

3 { } Bedrooms

2 { } Bedrooms

4 { } Kitchen,
Dining
Library

Living Room

Entrance

122. Schinkel House. 2nd variant. 1980

124

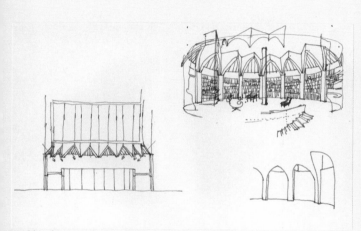

193. Schinkel House 2nd variant 1980

124. Schinkel House End pavant 1408

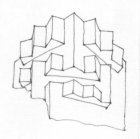

125. Schinkel House 2nd version 1980

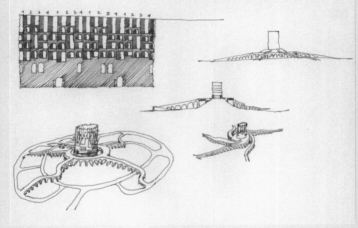

137. Steinkel House 2nd variant 1981

128

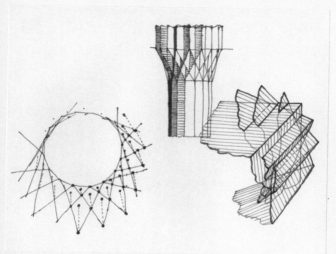

129. Schinkel House 2nd variant 1980

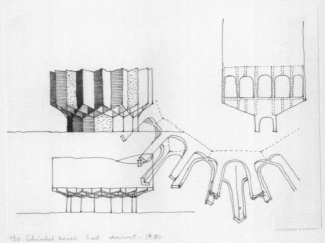

130. Schinkel House 2nd variant - 1980

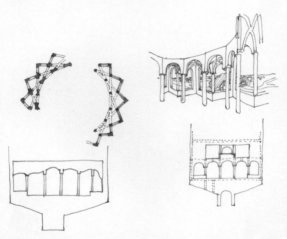

81. Schinkel House 2nd variant 1880

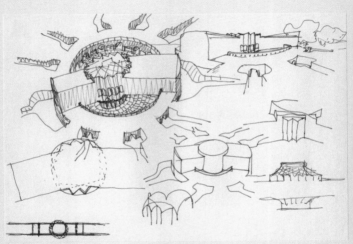

138 Schinkel Szene 2nd variant 1980

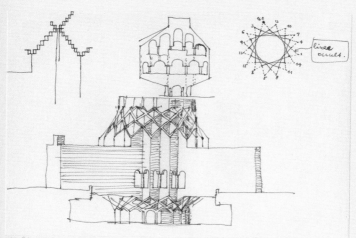

139. Schinkel house 2nd variant 1:4.80

linea occult.

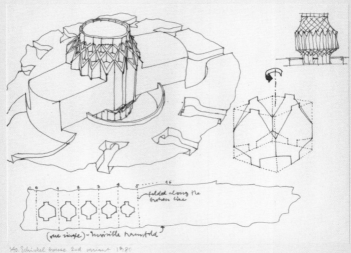

folded along the broken line

(one single) - invisible turn fold

142. Schinkel House 2nd variant 1980

134

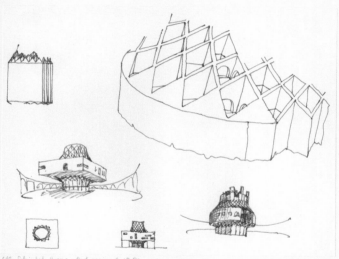

142. Schinkel House 2nd variant 10.80

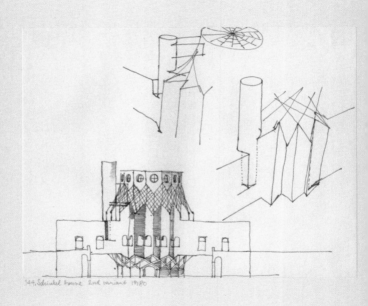

144. Schinkel House 2nd variant 1980

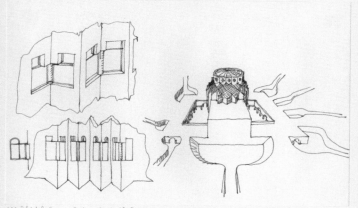

146. Schinkel House 2nd variant 10/80

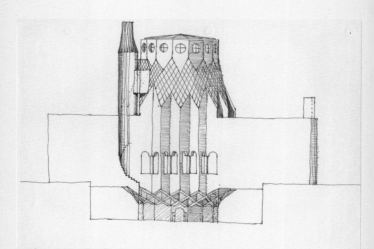

148. Schinkel Annexe 2nd variant 1:1'80

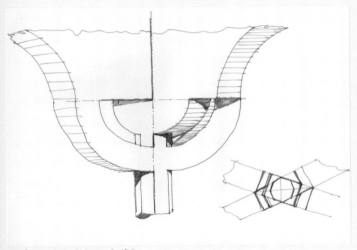

160. Schinkel House, 2nd variant. 1980

139

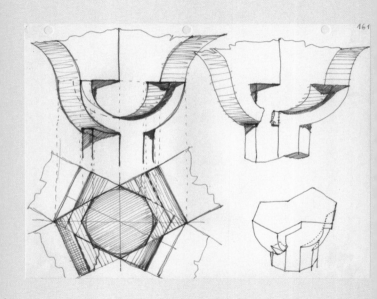

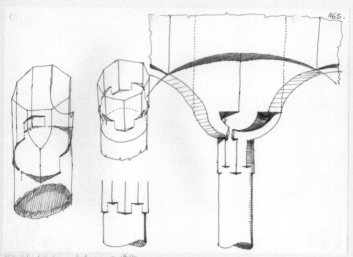

163. Schénkel frieze 2nd variant 19,80

141

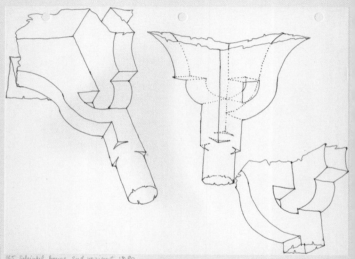

165. Schinkel house 2nd variant 1980

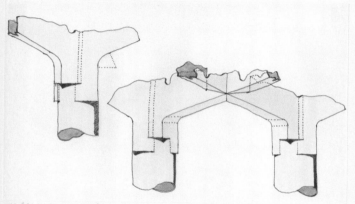

236 Schinkel house – second variant 19.81

237. Schinkel House - second variant 19,81

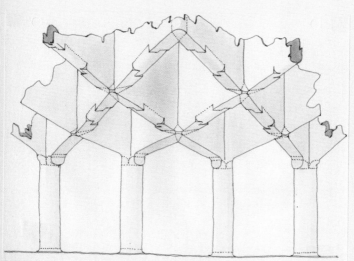

298 Celestial House—second version 1981

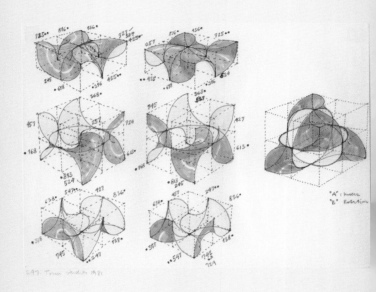

"A" : Inverse
"B" : Rotation

547 Truss studies 1981

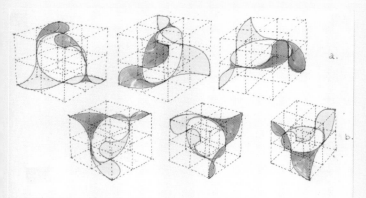

a.

b.

248. Torus fragments 1981

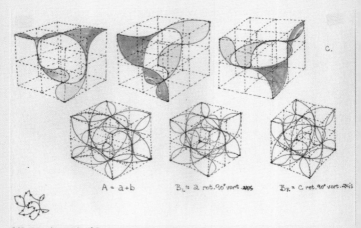

A = a + b   B_L = a rot. 90° vert. axis   B_R = c rot. 90° vert. axis

C.

249. Torus fragments 1981

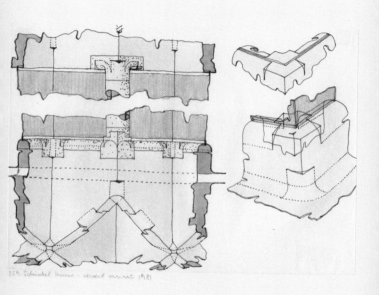

259. Schinkel house - second variant 1981

149

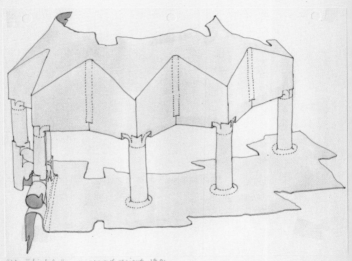

261. Schinkel House - second variant 1981

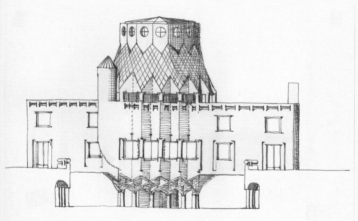

262. Schinkel House - second variant 1981

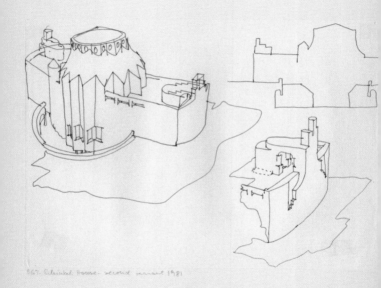

867. Schinkel House - second version 1981

152

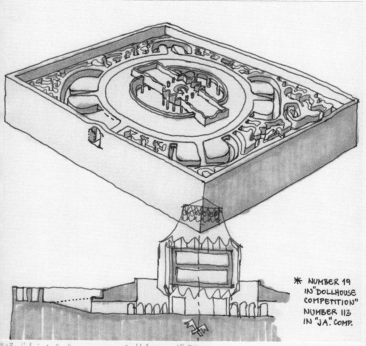

313. Schinkel House — as Doll house 1982

* NUMBER 19 IN "DOLLHOUSE COMPETITION" NUMBER 113 IN "J.A." COMP.

314. Schinkel House - an Doll House. 1982.

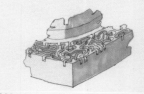

315. Schinkel House - an Doll House. 1982.

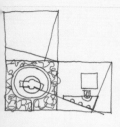

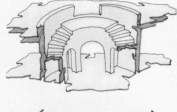

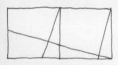

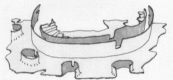

617. Schinkel House - second project 1833

9. Schinkel House - east and west views with Bell towers 1832

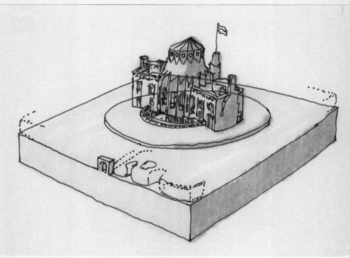

321. Schinkel House - as Doll House - second variant 1982

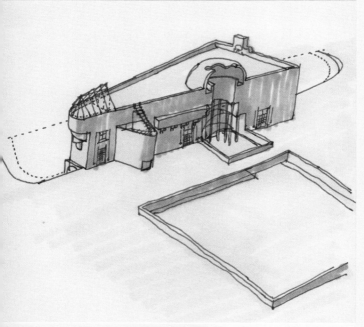

124. Schinkel House – first variant 1982

325. Schinkel House – first variant 1982

356. Schinkel House – second variant 1982

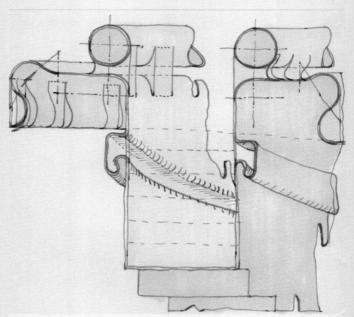

354. Schinkel House – second variant 1982

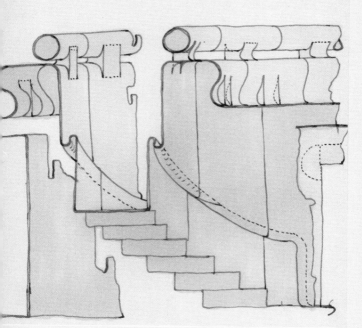

J.S. Schinkel House – second variant 1982

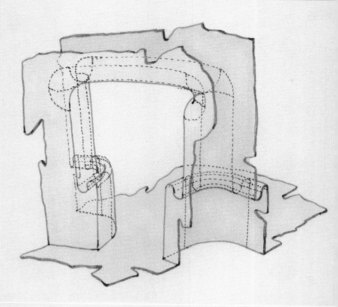

358. Schinkel House – second variant 1982

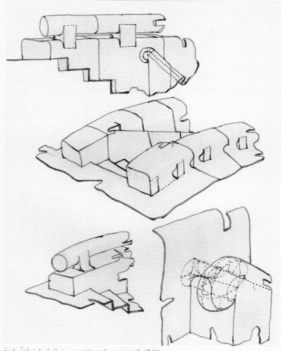

361. Schinkel House – second variant 1982

163

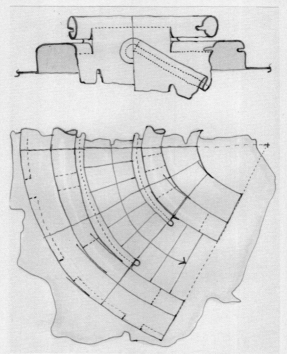

362 Schinkel House - second variant 1982

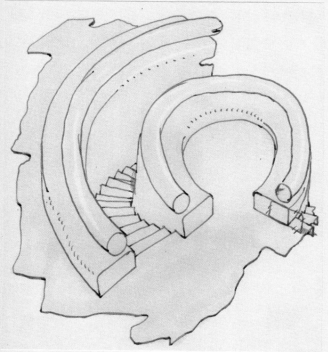

365. Schinkel House – second variant 1982

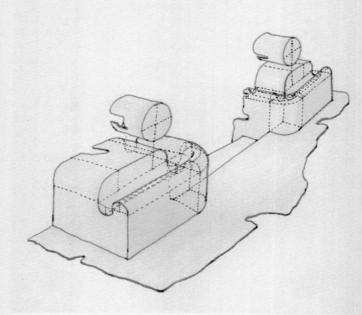

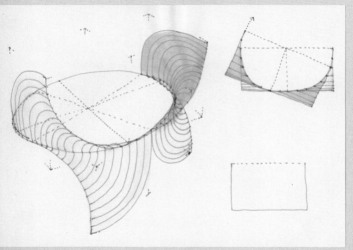

91. Schinkel House – second variant / geometrical studies 1982

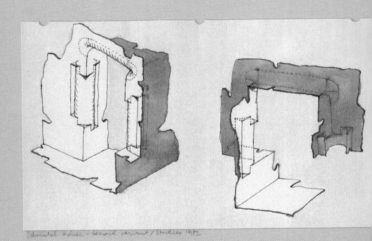

Schinkel House – second variant / Studies 1982

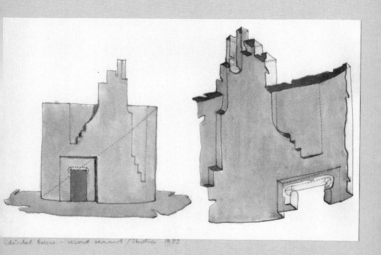

Steinbel House – second variant / studies 1982

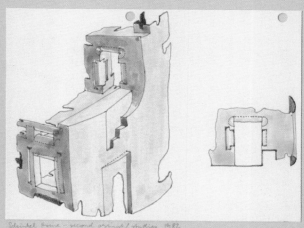

Schindel house — second project / studies 1982

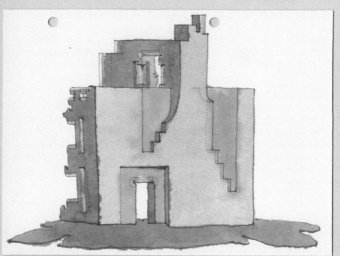

Schindel House – second variant / Study 1982.

New Architecture School

As a fictive finger-exercise, after appointed as the founding director of this school, part of the Florida Atlantic University in Fort Lauderdale, I ventured to answer my self-imposed question, what should be the locus for the education of architects? In reality, there was intent to build such a building, with public/private money, containing additional offices for different, university related spaces. After several site-related investigations, my personal memories of the African "Teaching-Tree" offered the beginnings of the solution, with massive trunk and branches above. This simplistic image was enriched by the application of two major forces in taming gravity, the tensional and compressive structures. In-between these I proposed a "neutral" space, an elevated public plaza, which separated the architectural school below, and the other functions above. All spaces were surrounded by a narrow walkway, which enabled the simple operation of the wooden louvers, protecting the openable glass walls. The studios and other areas formed a square-shaped ring around the cylindrical shaft of the vertical circulation. The remaining triangular areas were open above so the vertical airflow and the openable internal windows enabled the use of natural cross-ventilation of the spaces.

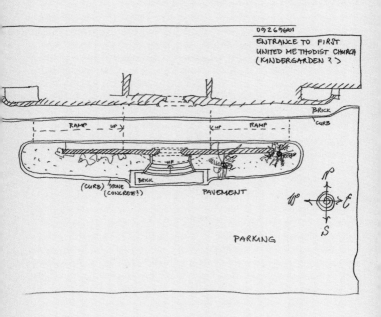

09269601

ENTRANCE TO FIRST
UNITED METHODIST CHURCH
(KINDERGARDEN ?)

BRICK
CURB

RAMP   UP →   ↑ UP   RAMP

(CURB) STONE
        (CONCRETE?)   PAVEMENT

UP

BRICK

N
W   E
S

PARKING

173

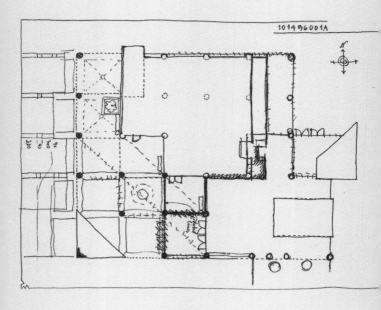

101496001A

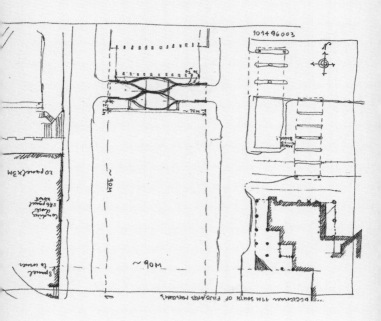

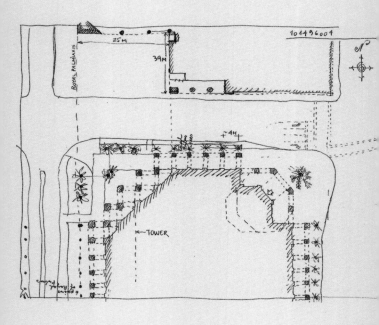

ROYAL PALM AXIS

25 M

39 M

101436004

N

4M

KIOSK

TOWER

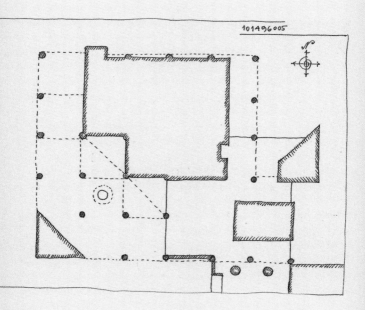

101496005

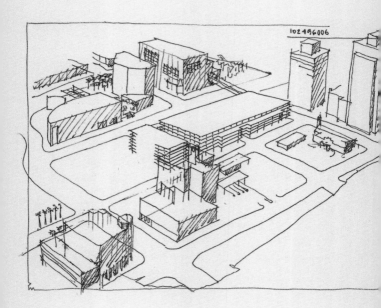

102496006

178

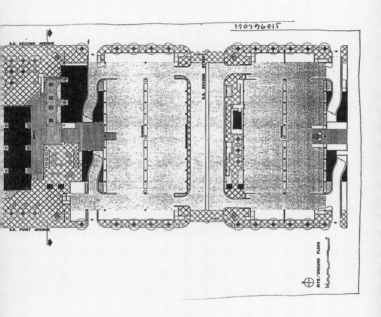

170776015

S.E. SECOND AVENUE

S.E. SECOND STREET

S.E. FIRST AVENUE

SITE / GROUND FLOOR

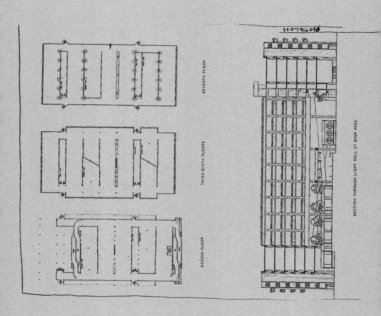

SEVENTH FLOOR

THIRD-SIXTH FLOORS

SECOND FLOOR

110796016

SECTION THROUGH LIGHT WELL AT SHOP AREA

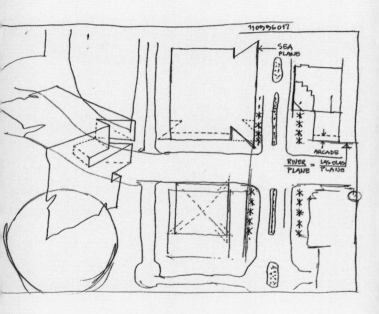

SEA PLANE

RIVER PLANE = LAS OLAS PLANE

ARCADE

110336017

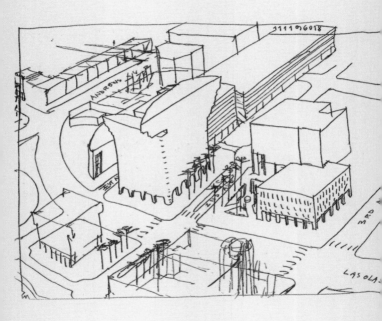

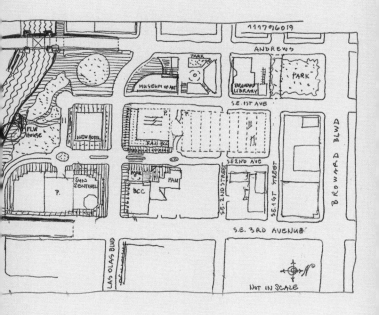

NOT IN SCALE

183

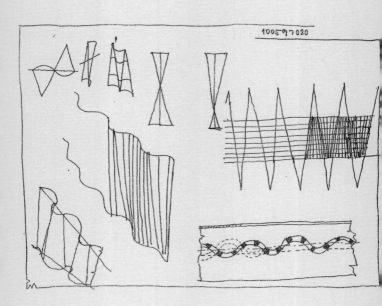

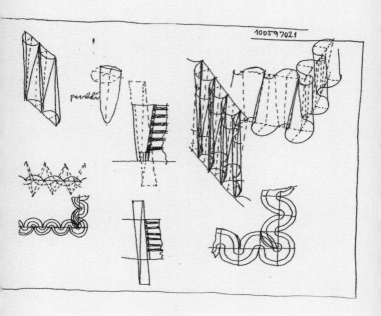

parabola

100597021

185

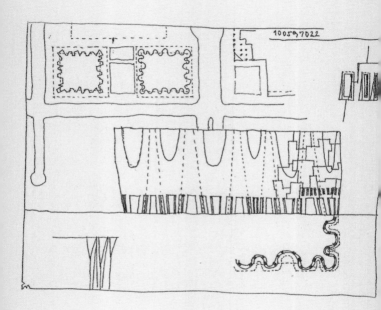

100597022

186

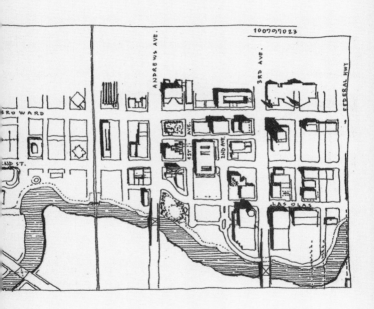

187

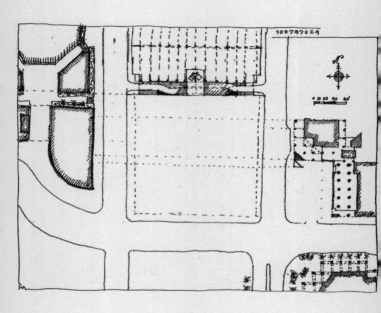

100797624

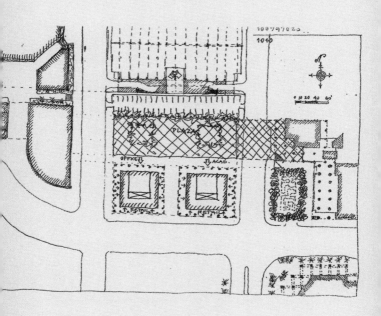

PLAZA

OFFICE

ACAD.

RETAIL   RETAIL

100 50 0 25

10'

0 10 20 40 60'

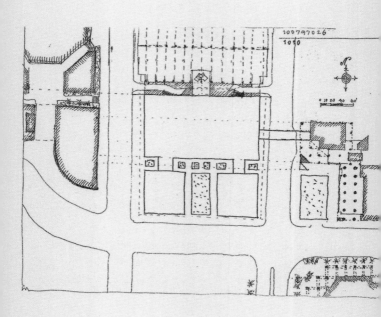

100797026
1050

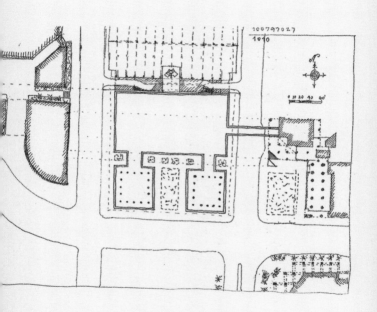

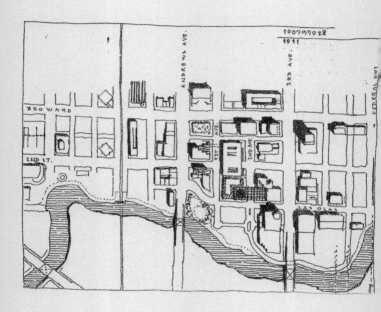

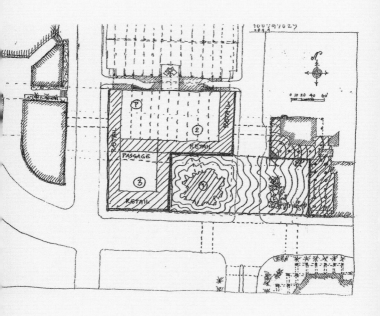

PASSAGE

RETAIL

RETAIL

193

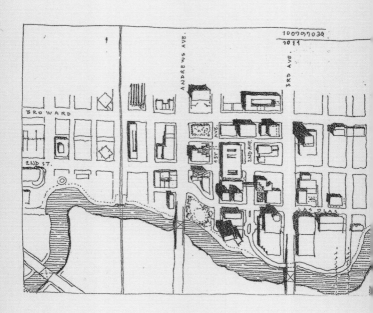

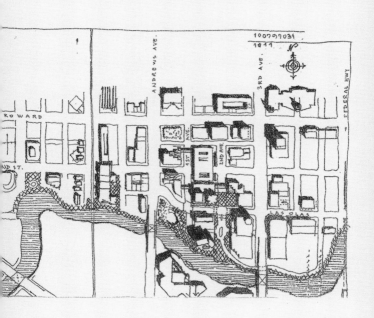

195

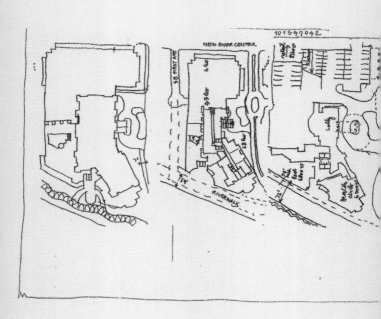

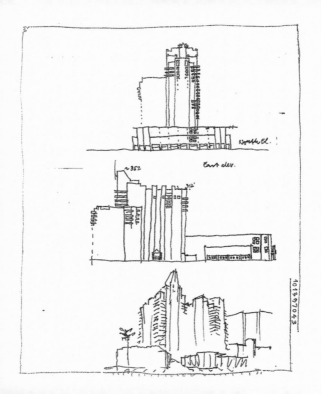

North El.

East elev.

~352

~312

10139704 3

197

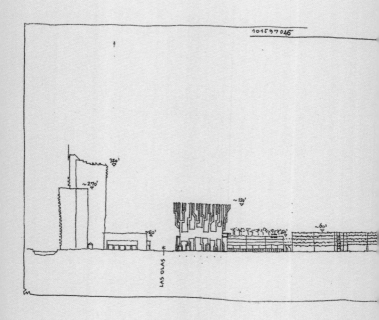

101597045

380'

~270'

250'

~130'

~60'

LAS OLAS

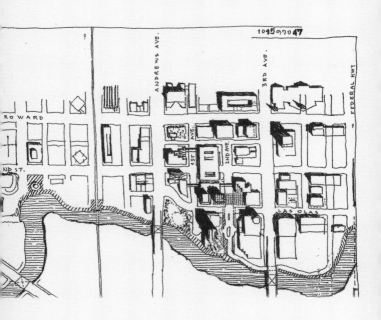

199

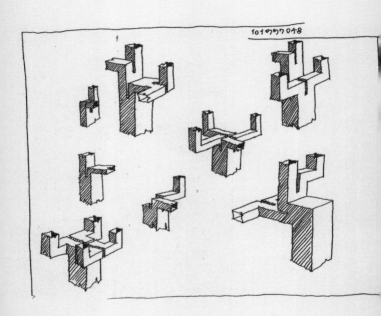

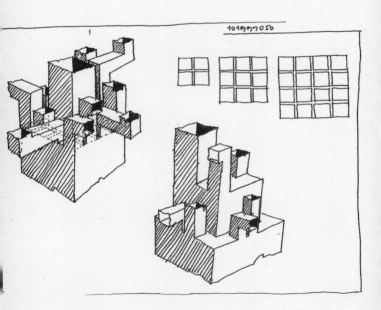

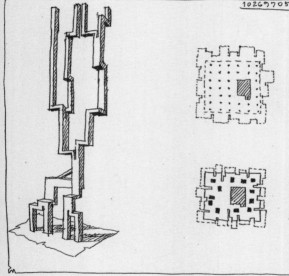

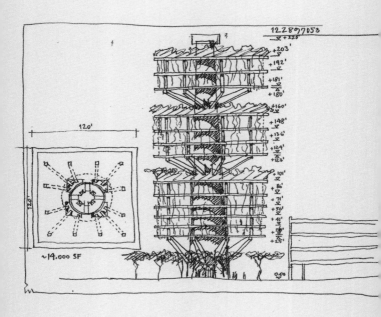

120'

~14,000 SF

122897053

+203'
+192'
+181'
+180'
+160'
+148'
+136'
+124'
+123'
+101'
+86'
+76'
+58'
+41'

0.00

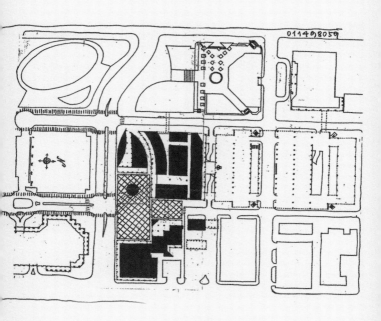

205

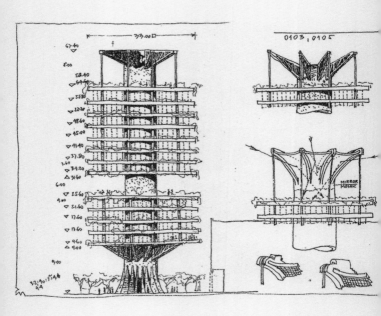

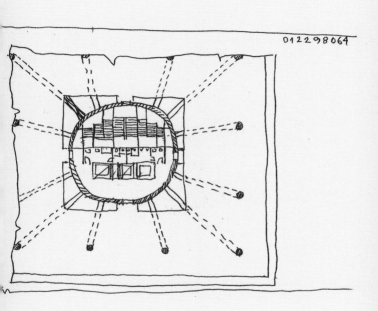

012298064

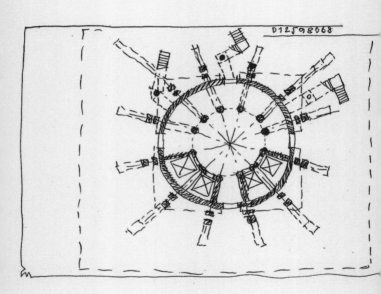

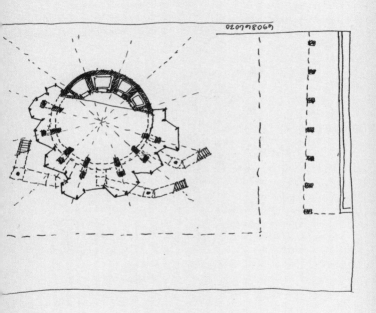

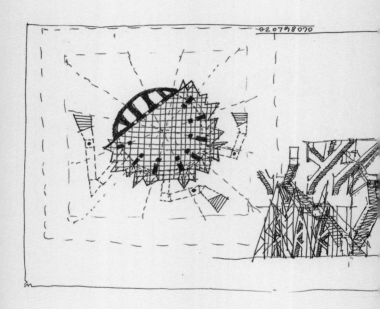

020798070

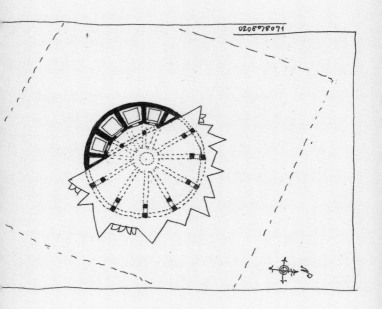

0208918071

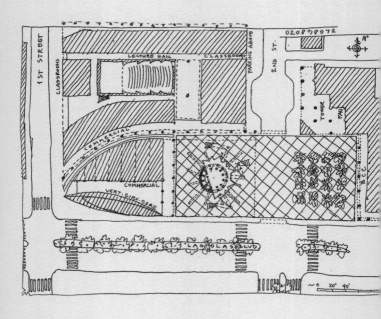

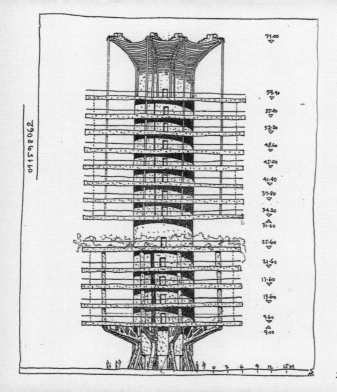

71·00

57·40
55·40
52·20
48·60
45·00
41·40
37·80
34·20
31·60

25·60

21·60
17·60
13·60
9·60
9·00

0 3 6 9 12 15 M

213

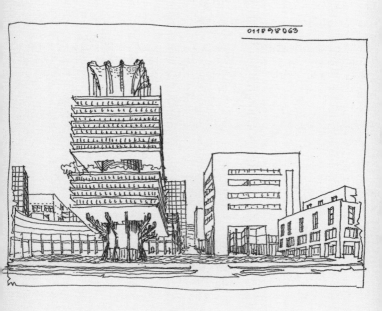

011898063

House With No Style

(Spiritual Retreat for Andrea Palladio and John Hejduk)

This competition, which was initiated and juried by Rem Kolhaas (and won by a project with no windows and doors), was later developed as a spiritual retreat for Andrea Palladio and John Hejduk. Through many transformations, it was reduced to the typologies of cells and a hall, connected by stairs to each other.

The relative proportions recalled Palladio, and the somewhat quirky stairs referenced Hejduk's projects. The final digital presentation is the work of my friend and former student, Scott Magar.

The project, in the theoretical, unbuilt category, received a merit award from the American Institute of Architects' Florida/Caribbean Chapter. The members of the international jury were Mr. Franco Purini, Ms. Laura Thermes, and Mr. Carlos Casuscelli. Here is an excerpt of their comment: "This proposal calls for a metaphysical space, where the functional aspects are reduced to complete abstraction. Architecture then becomes a poetical expression of unexpected stairs that are symbolic of human aspirations."

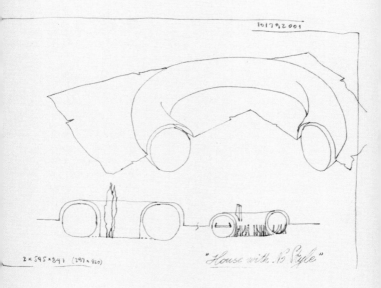

101792001

2 × 595 × 841 (297 × 420)

"House with 13 Style"

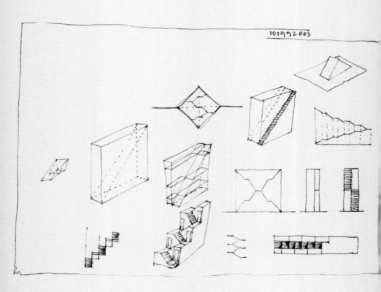

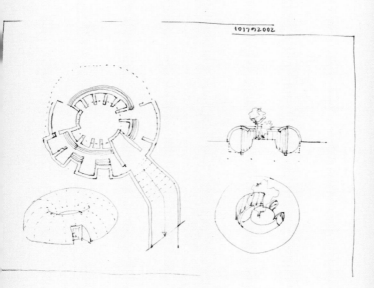

219

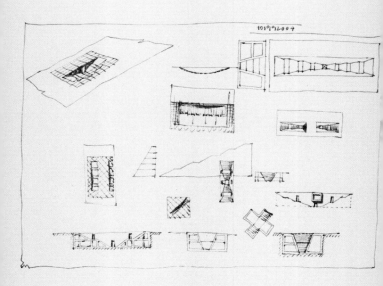

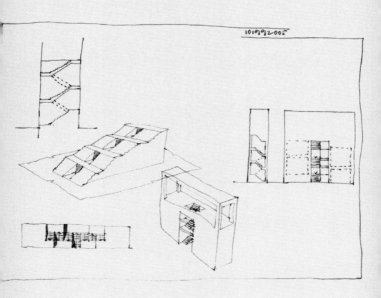

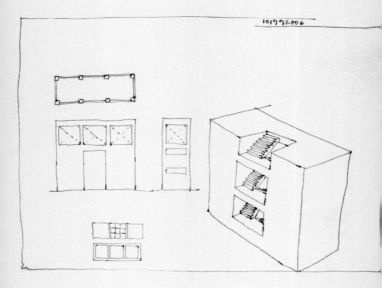

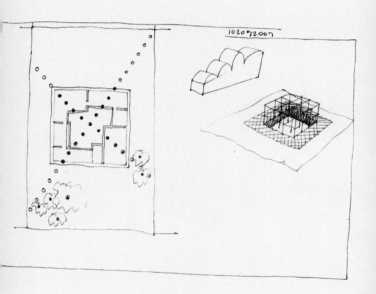

1020 7200 7

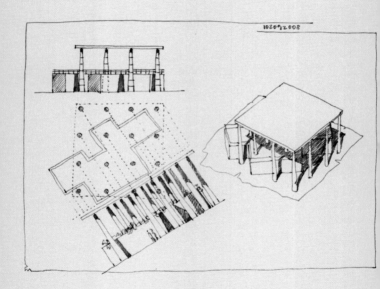

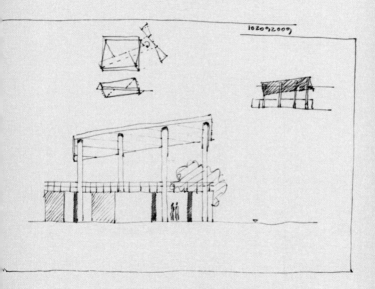

102032009

225

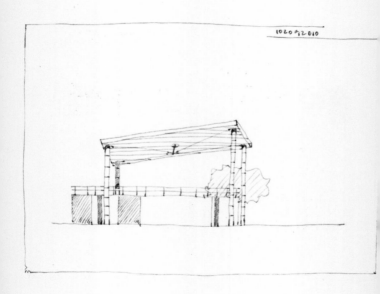

1020年2010

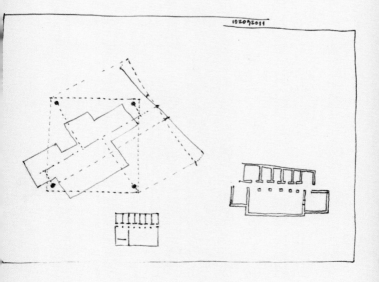

227

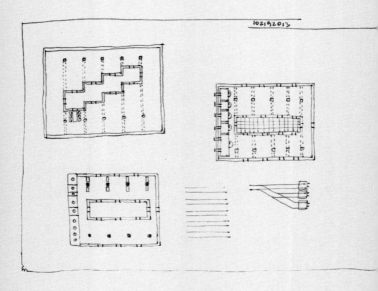

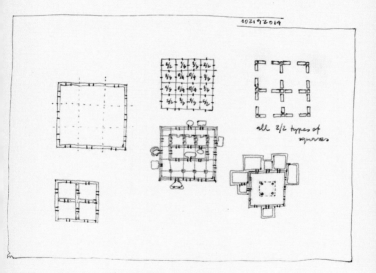

all 2/2 types of
squares

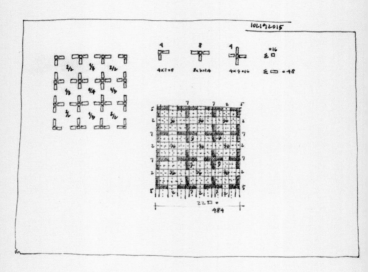

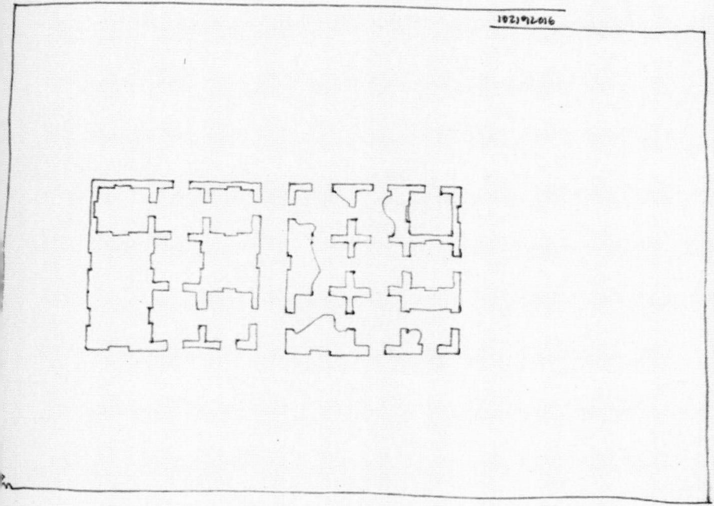

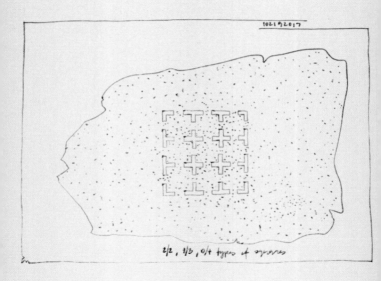

10217 92017

2/2, 1/3, 0/4 types of squares

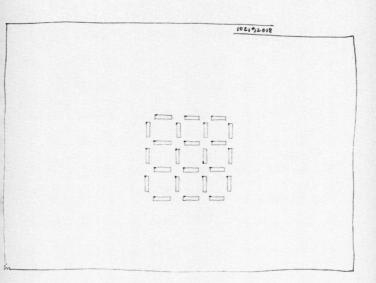

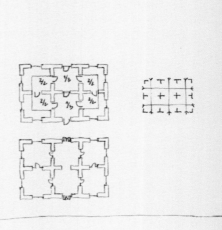

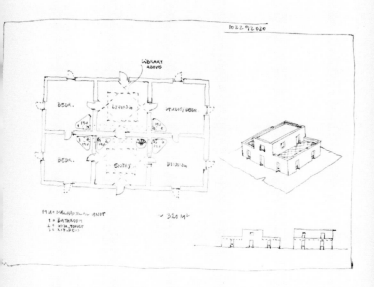

LIBRARY
ABOVE

BEDR.

LIVING

STUDIO/BEDR.

BEDR.

ENTRY

DINING

M A = MECHANICAL UNIT
1 = BATHROOM
2 = WSH, TOILET
3 = KITCHEN

~ 320 M²

235

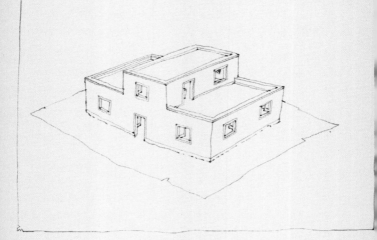

236

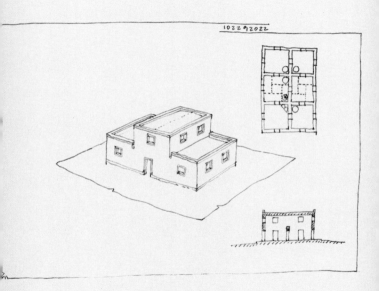

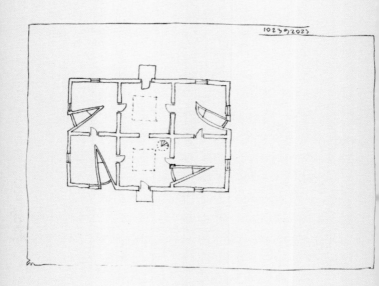

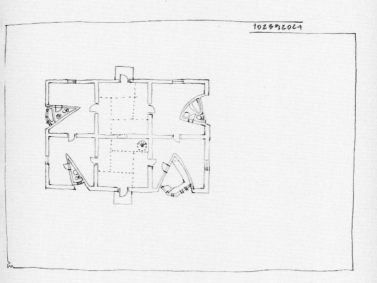

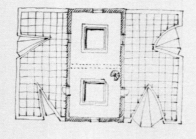

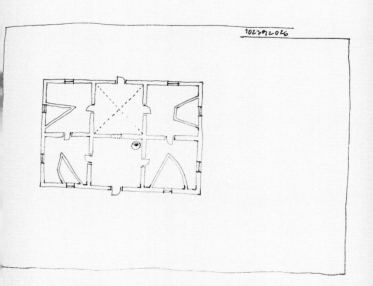

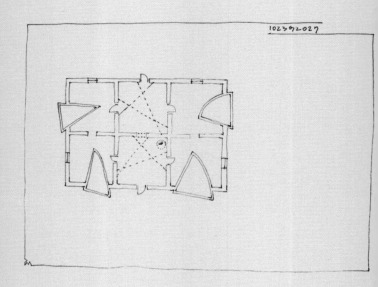

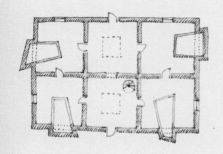

102372028

243

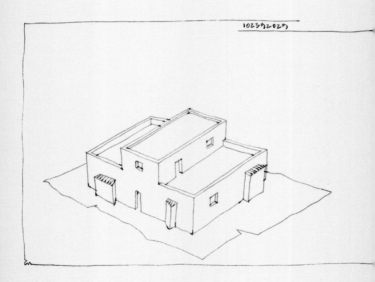

102392029

244

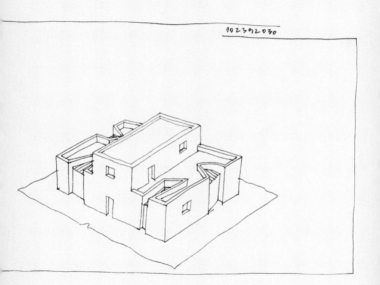

102392030

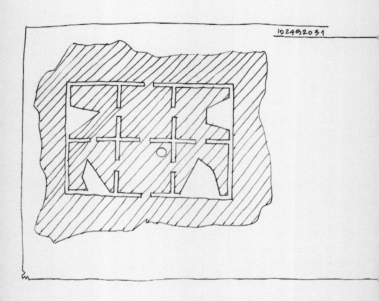

246

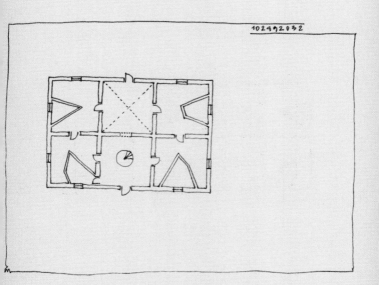

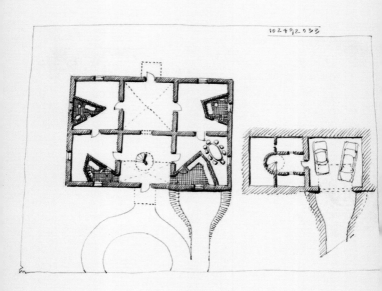

248

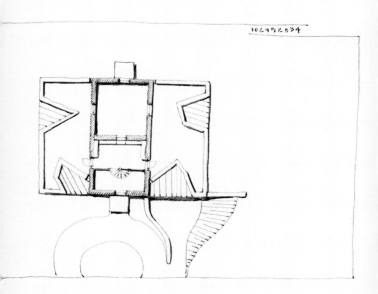

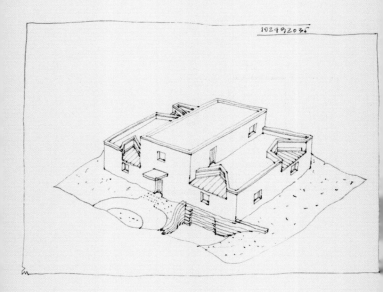

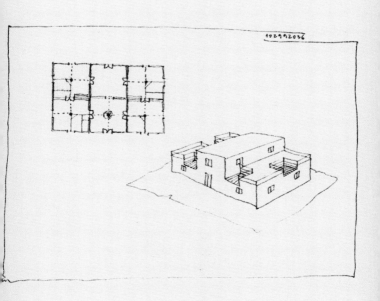

251

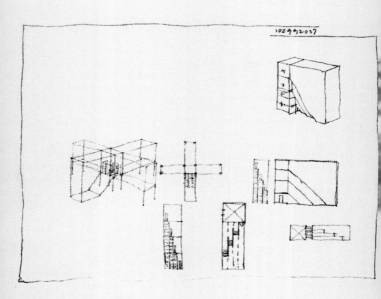

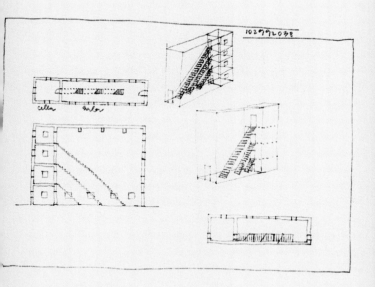

10279 2038

cella   Salor

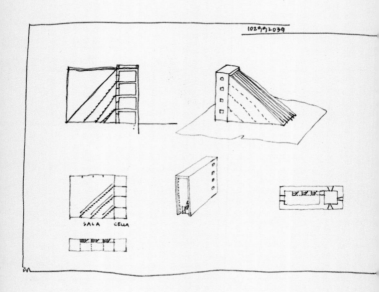

SALA CELLA

254

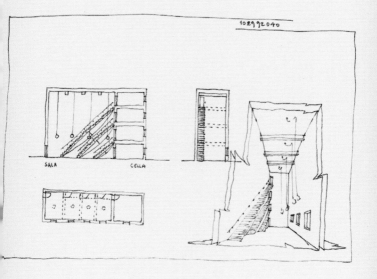

SALA   CELLA

255

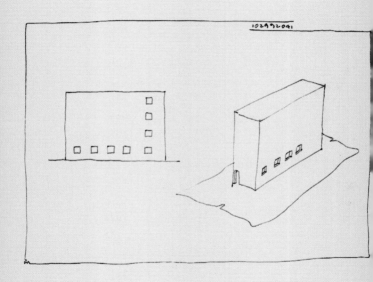

1029°32042

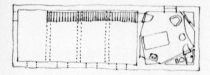

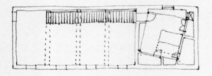

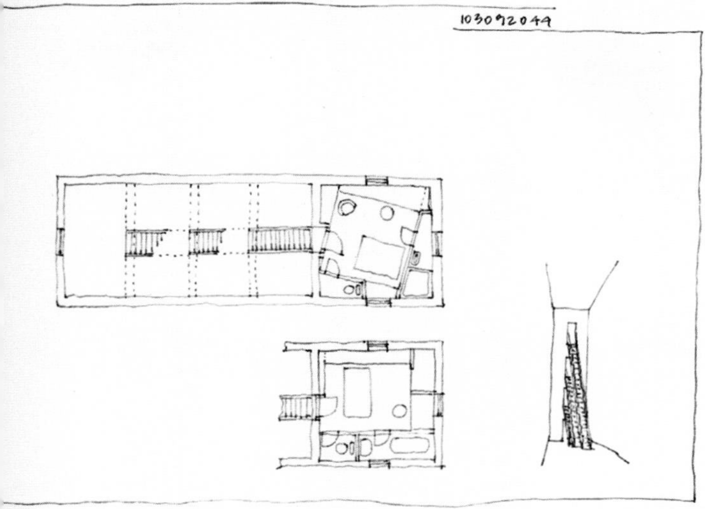
103092049

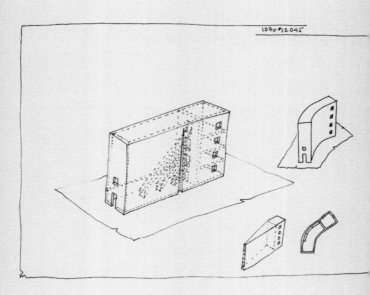

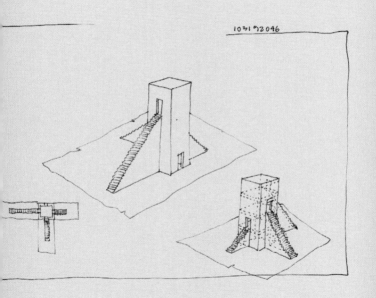

261

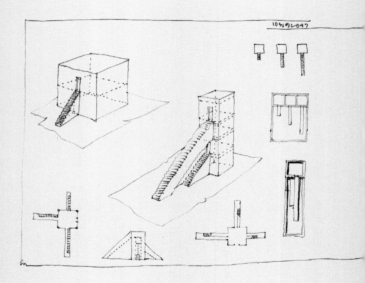

103102047

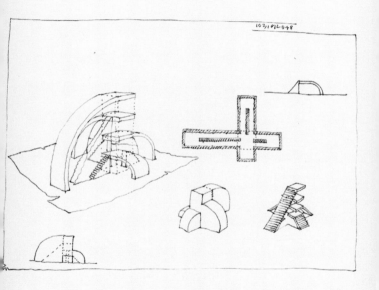

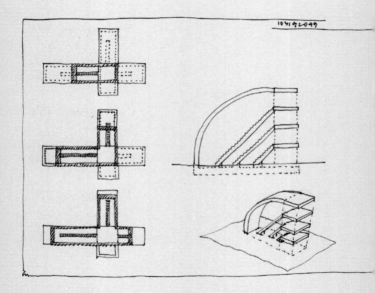

264

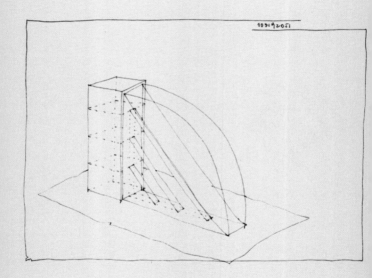

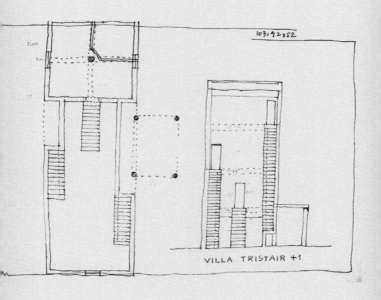

103192052

VILLA TRISTAIR +1

267

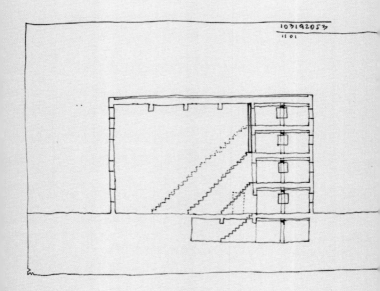

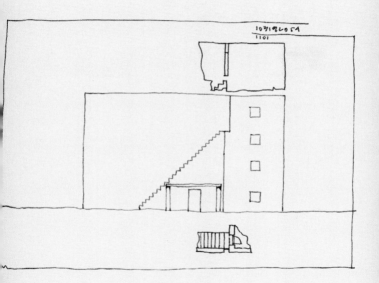

269

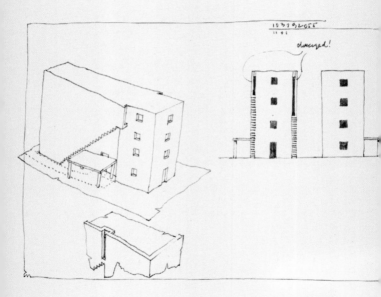

damaged!

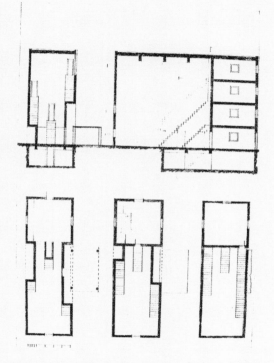

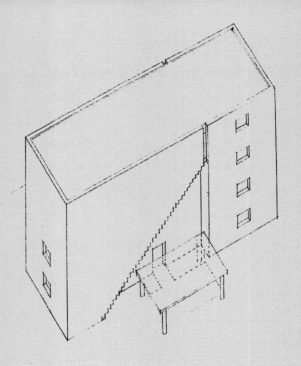

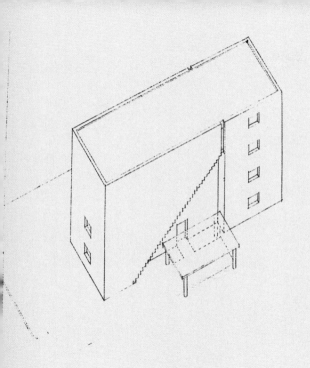

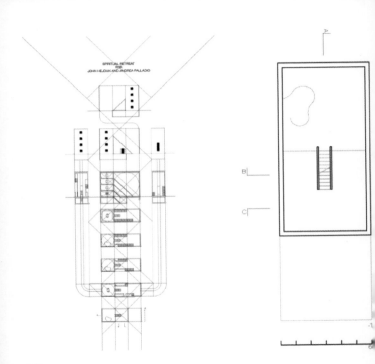

SPIRITUAL RETREAT
FOR
JOHN HEJDUK AND ANDREA PALLADIO

274

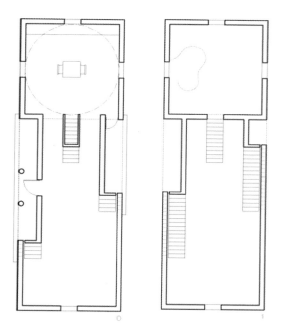

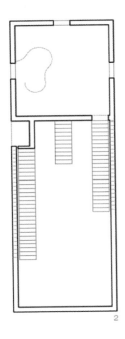 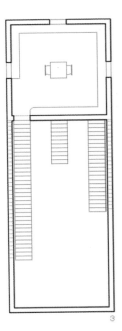

2   3

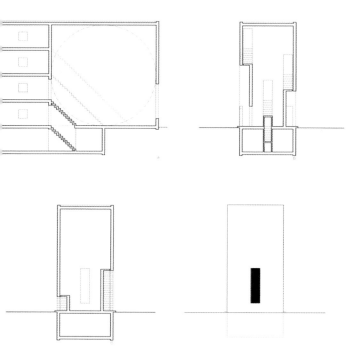

277

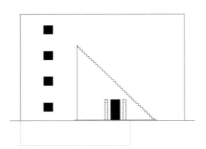

POPAMORTRAS

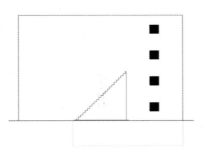

House for a Virtuoso, Venice

A particular moral excellence and great technical skills in the practice of fine arts: these are the definitions of virtue and virtuosity, respectively. In this spirit I was invited to design a house in Venice, Italy, for a retiring violin virtuoso, who has been honored by the citizens of Venice with the most precious gift: a piece of land on the Grand Canal.

The virtuoso (as with angels, gender is unimportant) intended to withdraw from the limelight and public appearances, but wanted to teach a select group of master-class students. There was a limit established of seven pupils. They were to live elsewhere, but practice rooms, occasional concerts, and common meals in the master's house were part of their good fortune. The accommodation was to serve a convenient but non-pretentious life, where the search for spiritual value would go undisturbed by empty architectural gestures.

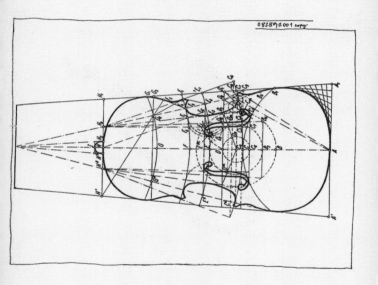

283

The modern violin

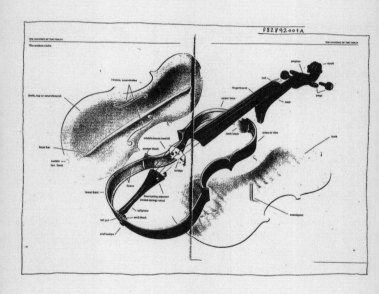

f-holes, soundholes

(belly, top or soundboard)

bass bar

saddle
ten feast

lower bout

fine-tuning adjuster
(metal strings only)

tailpiece

tail gut

end button

end block

fibres

bridge

upper block

middle bouts (waist)

scroll

pegbox

nut

fingerboard

upper bout

neck

neck block

sides or ribs

back

soundpost

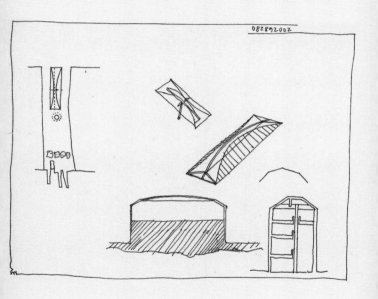

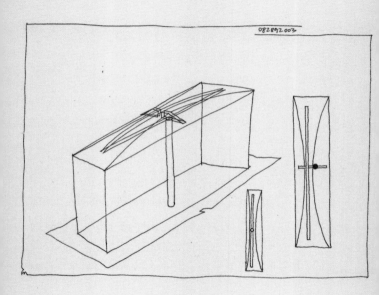

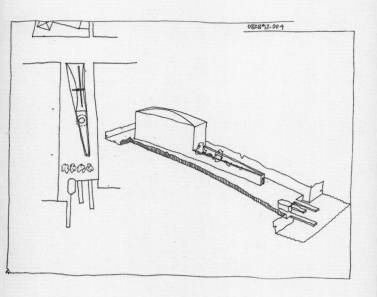

082892-004

287

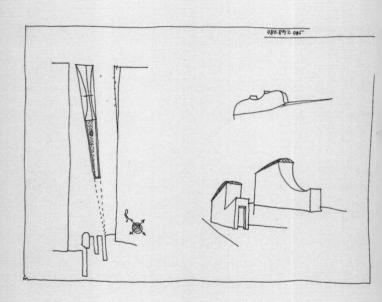

082892 085

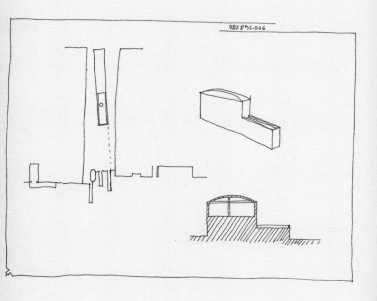

082892-006

289

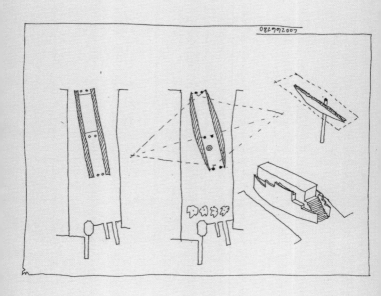

290

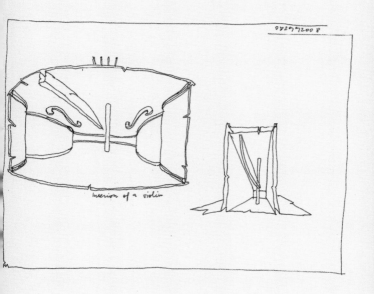

Interior of a violin

291

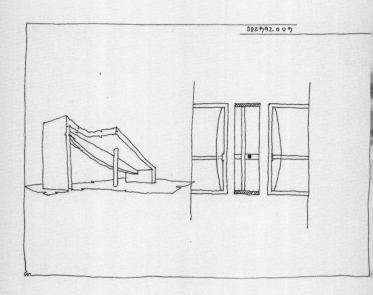

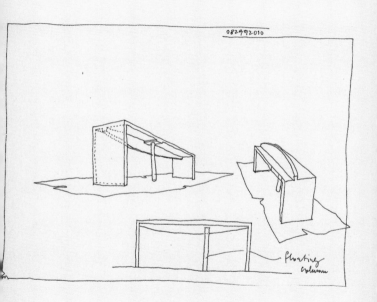

floating
column

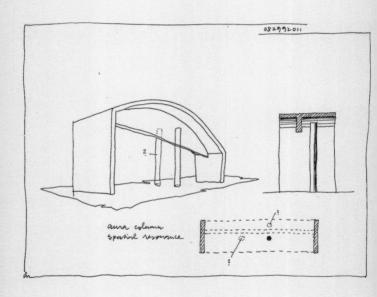

aura column
spatial resonance

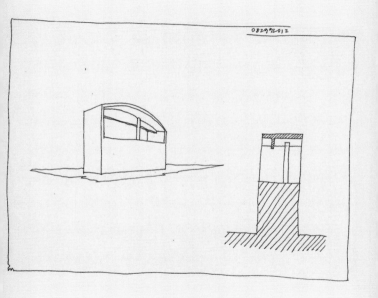

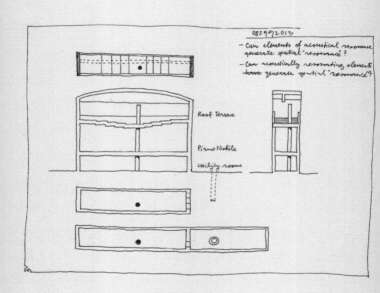

0829092013

- Can elements of acoustical resonance generate spatial "resonance"?
- Can acoustically resounding elements have generate spatial "resonance"?

Roof Terrace

Piano Nobile

Utility rooms

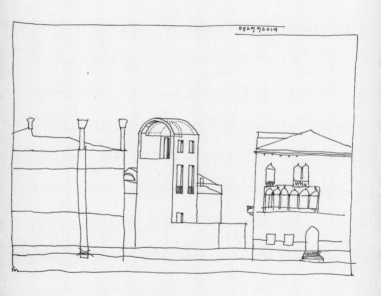

082972014

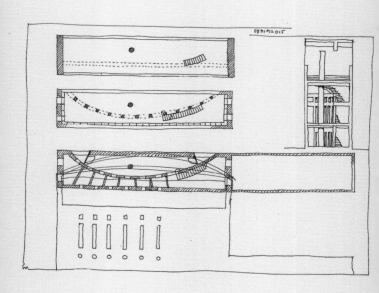

08.10.2015

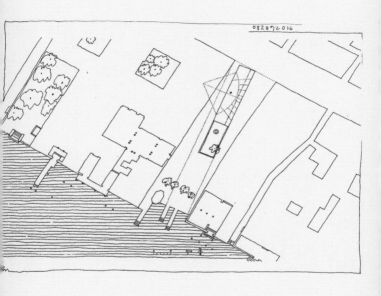

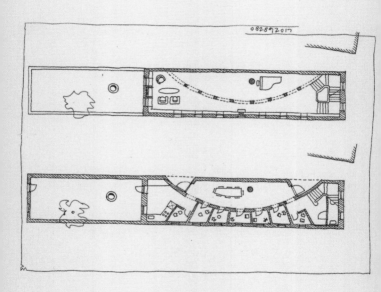

082897 2017

300

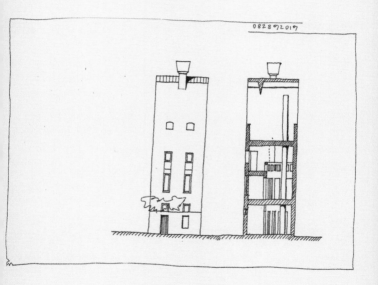

301

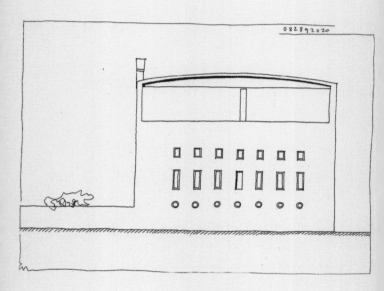

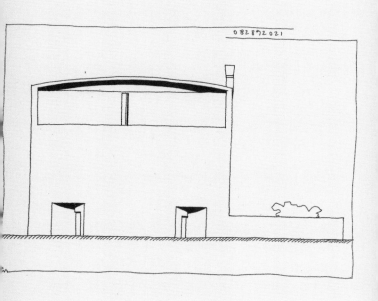

082892021

303

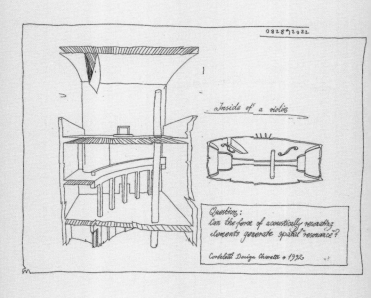

0828⁷2022

Inside of a violin

Question:
Can the form of acoustically resonating
elements generate spatial resonance?

Corbeletti Design Chiaretti * 1992

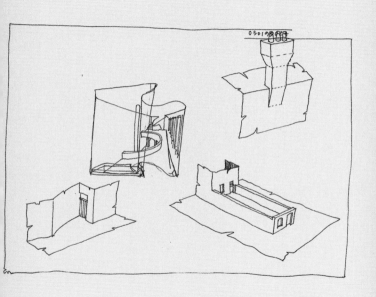

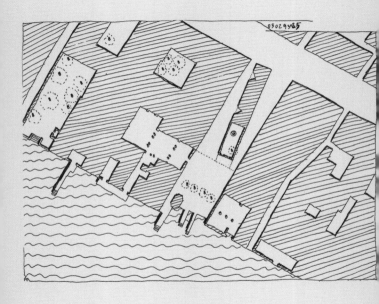

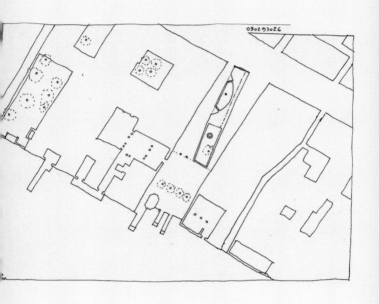

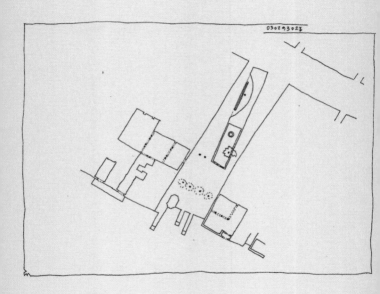

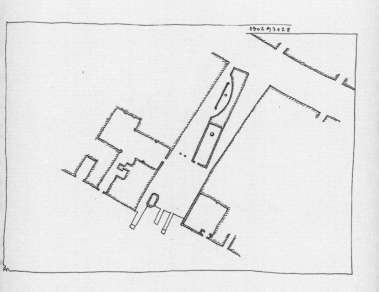

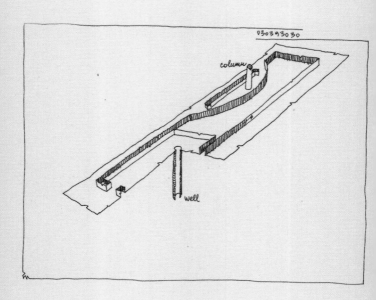

column

030393030

well

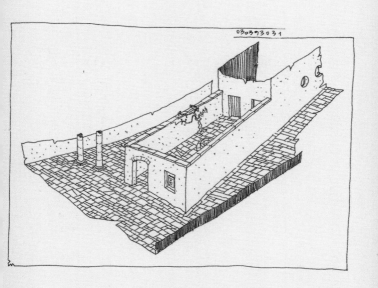

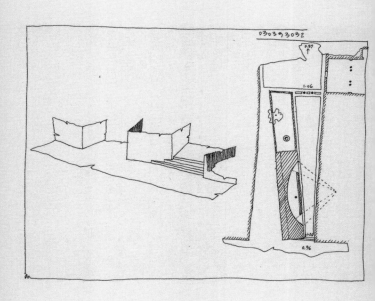

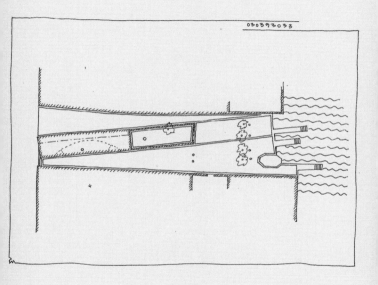

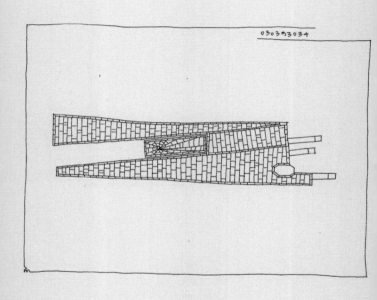

314

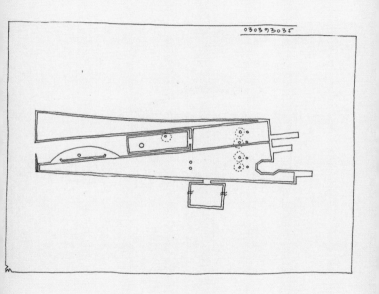

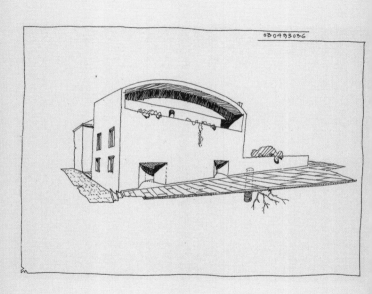

030493036

316

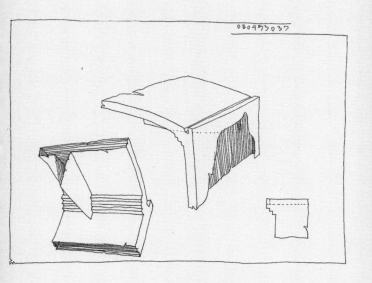

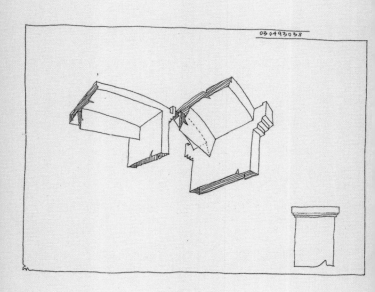

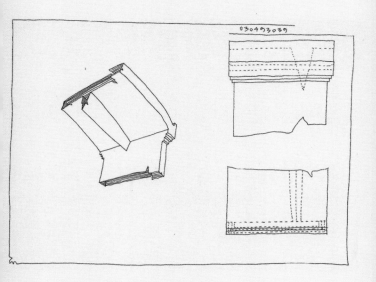

0304 3039

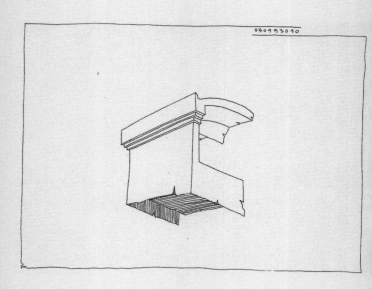

320

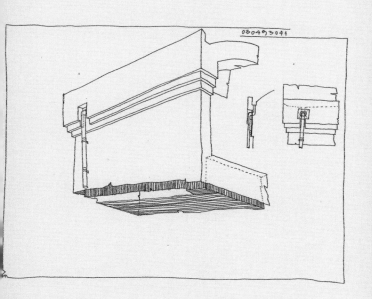

03040930041

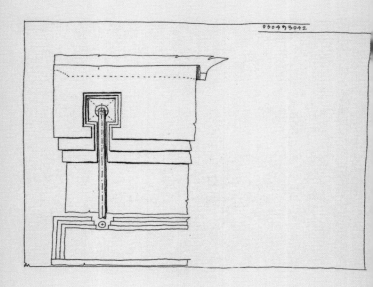

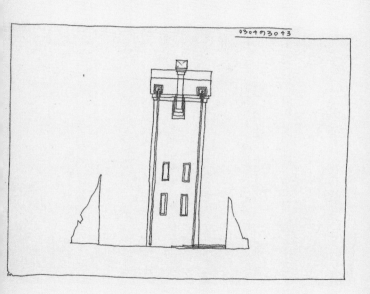

03049 3043

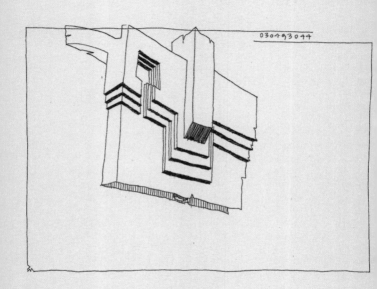

030493044

he Peggy Guggenheim Museum, Venice

The project was suggested by the late Aldo Rossi, and this submission was shown on the nice Biennale. This idea-competition was supposed to investigate the rare opportunity to build a w building along the Grand Canal in Venice, Italy.

e Leoni Family had a lofty plan for the site – to build a grand Renaissance palace. The construction rted, the lion heads—the family symbol—were placed on the sea wall and the columns, which re part of the colonnaded entry, and along the wall facing the Canal. The bank collapsed, but the ite stone wall and columns survived.

They stood unfinished, representing unfulfilled intentions for centuries. Eventually Peggy ggenheim, the descendant of another grand family, purchased the site. Her art collection grew d new extensions were added, but even they were not large enough. Hence the fictional task to sign a twentieth-century palace, with all the opportunities and restrictions the site offered. Con- quently, after a short sequence of typological investigation of the Venetian palazzo, the designer's ention was focused on the details of the wall and the columns.

After several urban scale inquiries, the internal distribution of spaces was investigated. One the drawings recalled earlier involvement with corner types. There are two major kinds of corners: e where three ninety-degree plane-fragments intersect; the other where two ninety and one 0-degree fragment join.

The result was an infinitely repeatable surface, with two distinctly separated spatial domains. t one corner formation appears, the 90/90/270 degree kind. My belief is that among the many re- rch areas related to architecture, basic geometrical research, and resulting accidental discoveries, should be one of them. Regular geometrical formations are very rarely applicable to architecture, but their derivatives are. A mutated version of the space type described above was actualized for the given function. Due to the intersecting spaces, several sight lines would enrich the spatial experience of the building, while the peripheral openings intermingle the views of Venice with the views of the art pieces.

DARIO.   PALAZZETTO   PALAZZO CORNER DELLA   PALAZZO BARBAR
       PISANI   CA'GRANDE, J. SANSOVINO, 1537   XVII SEC.

LAZZO DUCALE, XIV SEC.   PONTE DEI SOSPIRI,   PALAZZO DELLE PRIGIONI,   PALAZZO DANDOLO, XV SEC.
                       A. CONTIN, 1603   A. DA PONTE, 1560

NTECOLO.   PALAZZO DARIO,   PALAZZO VENIER DEI LEONI,   PALAZZO DA MULA,   CAMPO S. VIO
C.   P. LOMBARDO, 1487   L. BOSCHETTI, 1749, INCOMPIUTO   XV SEC.

328

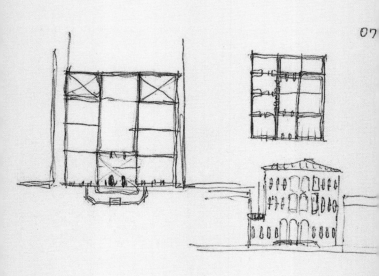

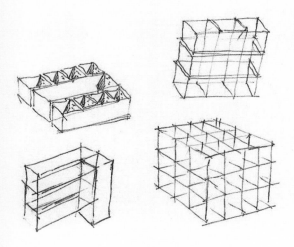

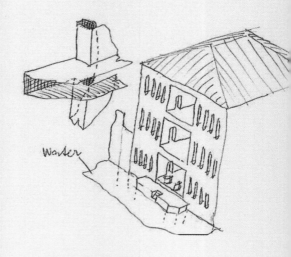

Water

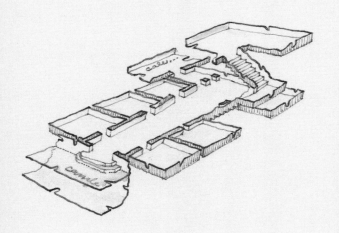

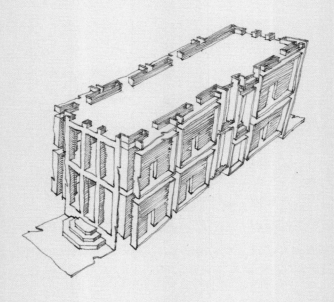

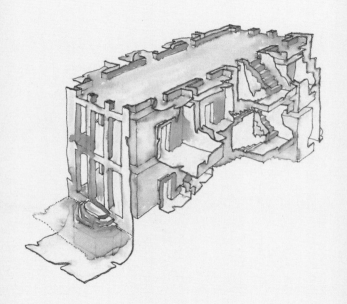

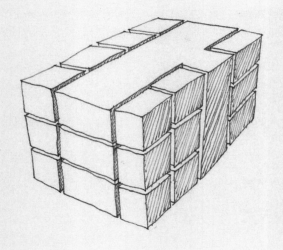

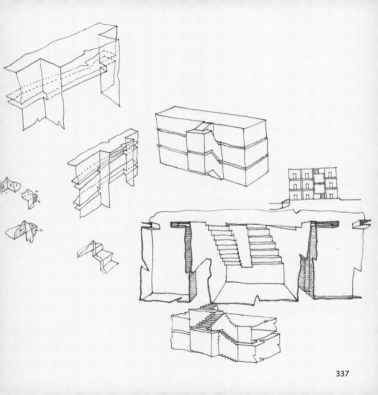

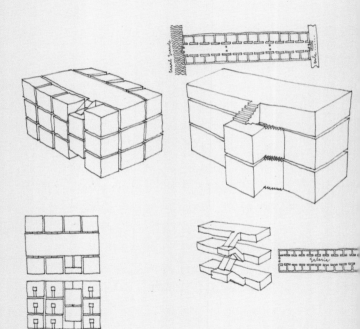

338

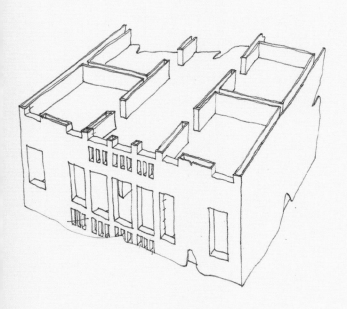

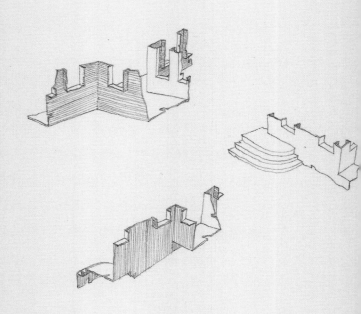

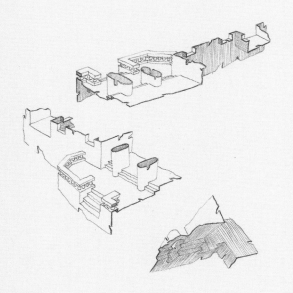

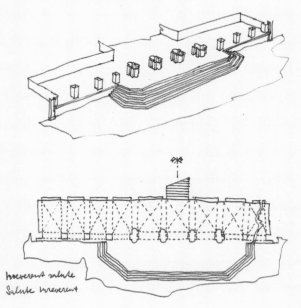

Irreverent salute
Salute irreverent

343

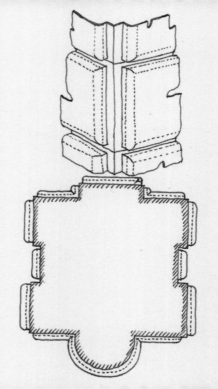

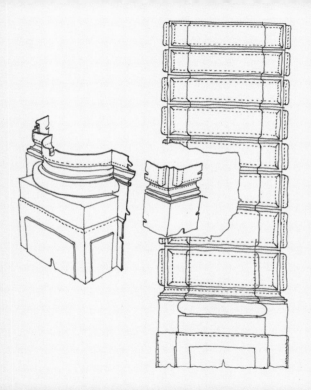

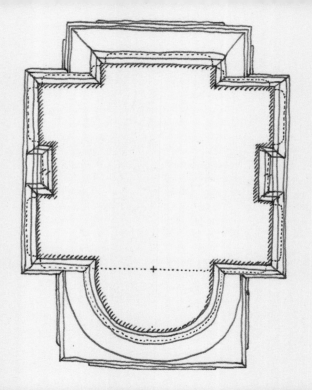

346

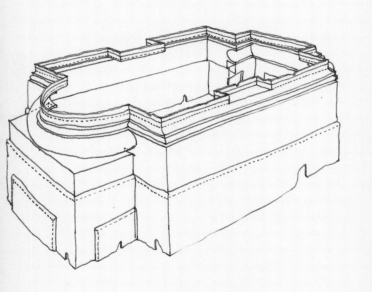

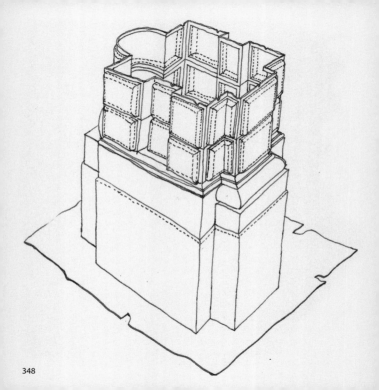

348

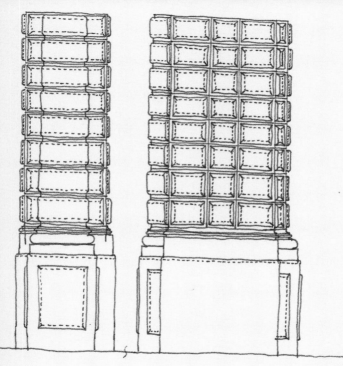

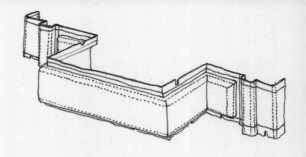

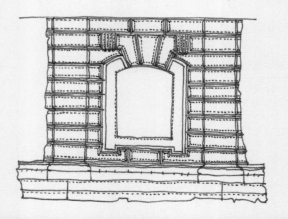

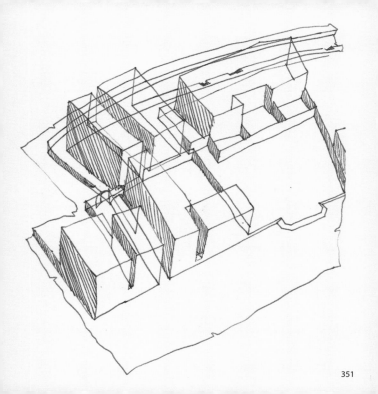

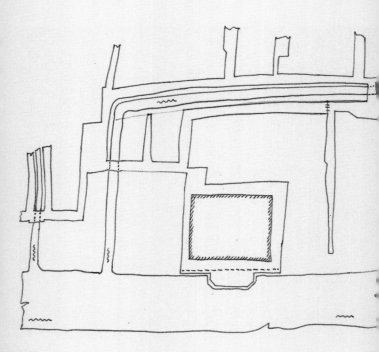

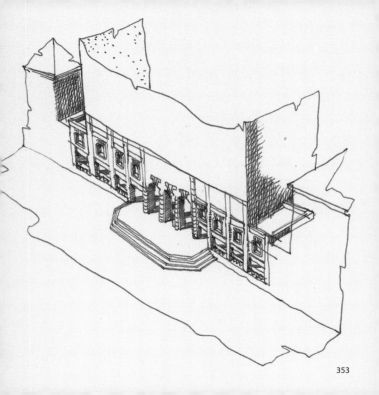

353

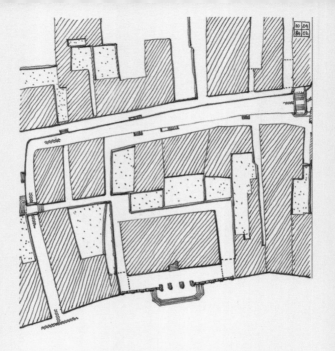

0   5   10   15   20 M

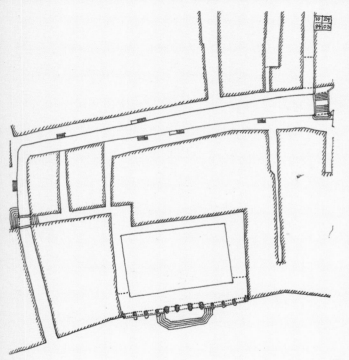

356

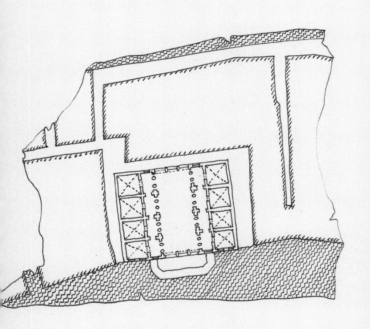

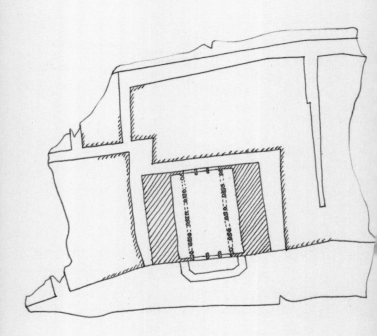

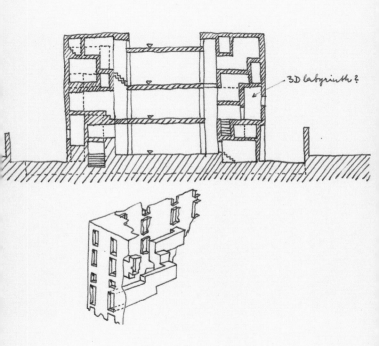

3D labyrinth?

359

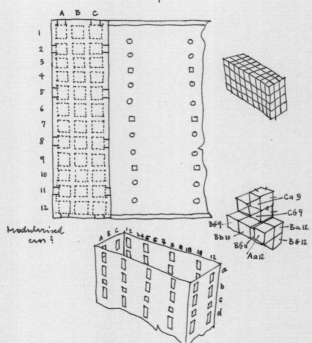

Modularized
cars ?

360

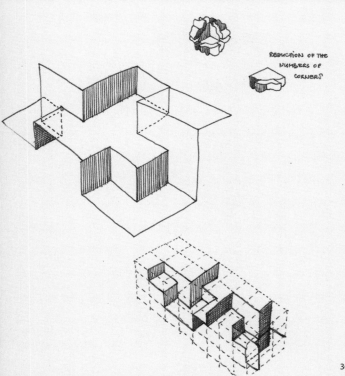

REDUCTION OF THE
NUMBERS OF
CORNERS

361

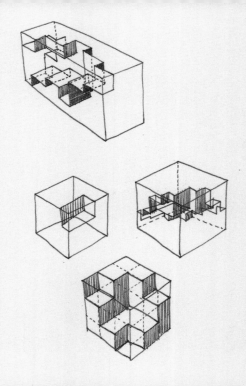

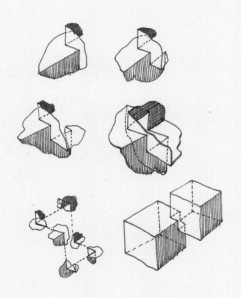

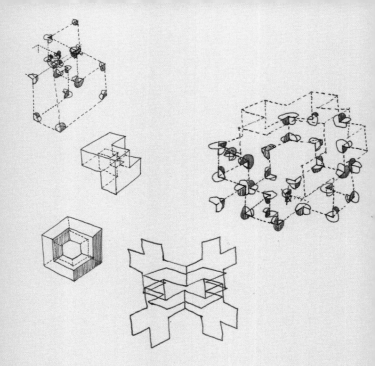

"HOLECUBE"
"CUBEHOLE"

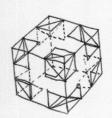

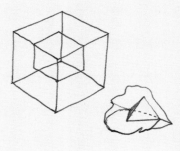

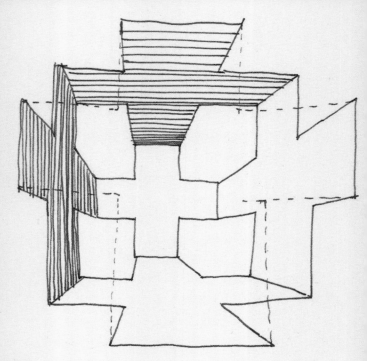

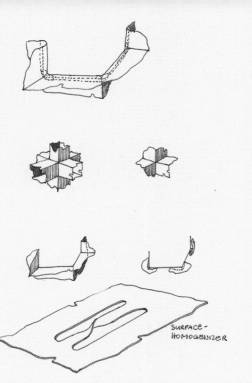

SURFACE-
HOMOGENIZER

367

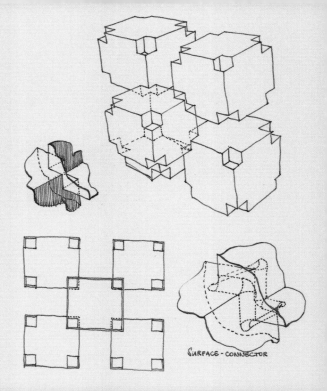

SURFACE - CONNECTOR

368

DETECTION
CHARACTERIZATION
CONTROL

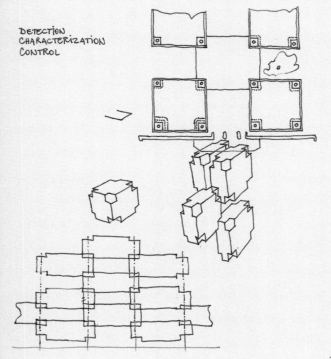

369

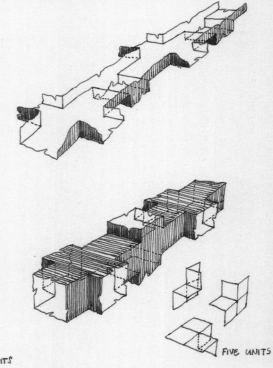

370　3 UNITS

FIVE UNITS

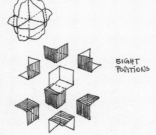

EIGHT POSITIONS

TWENTY-FOUR POSITIONS

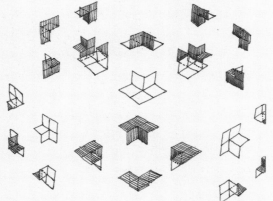

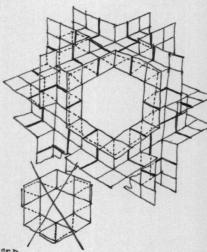

CUBE = 8 × 3 UNITS → CLOSED

"HOLECUBE" = 24 × 5 UNITS → OPEN STRUCTURE

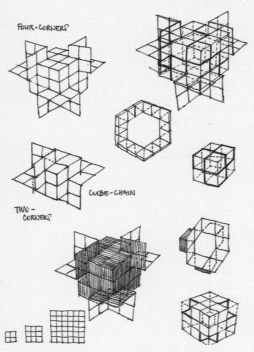

FOUR-CORNERS

CUBE-CHAIN

TWO-CORNERS

18 UNITS DOUBLE NEGATIVE "CORNER"

8×18 UNITS - "HOLECUBE"

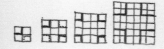

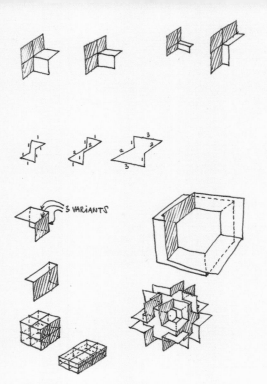

3 VARIANTS

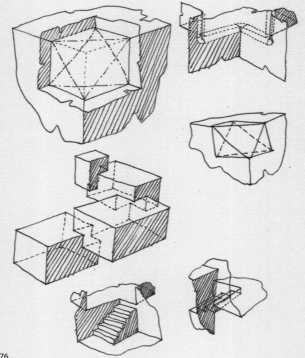

376

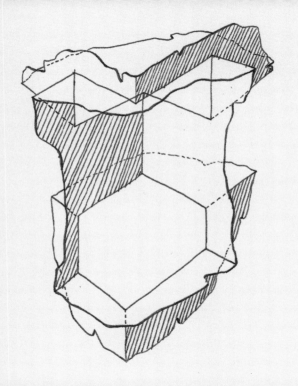

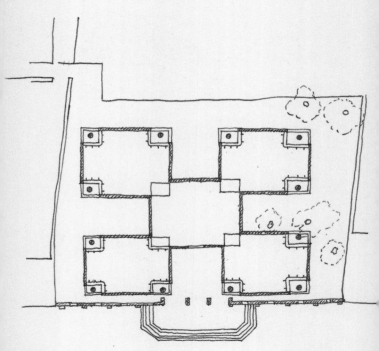

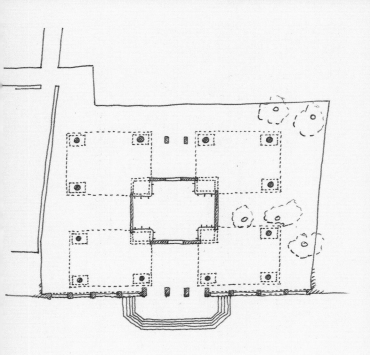

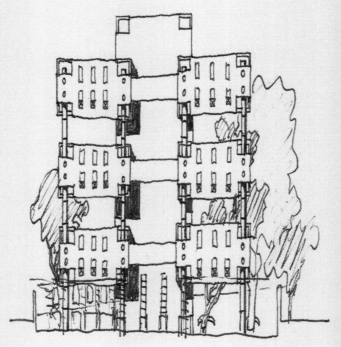

380

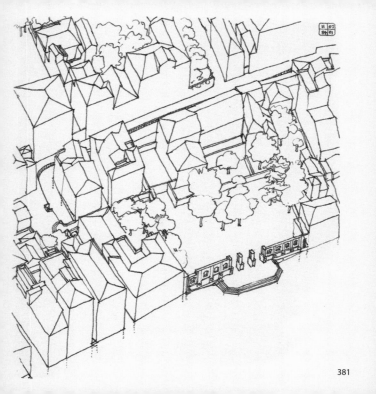

381

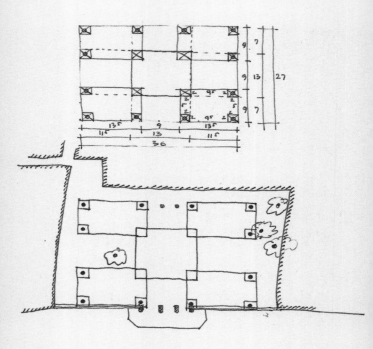

382

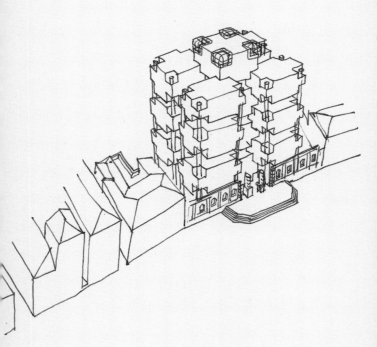

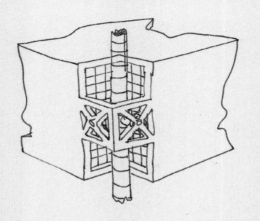

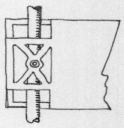

384

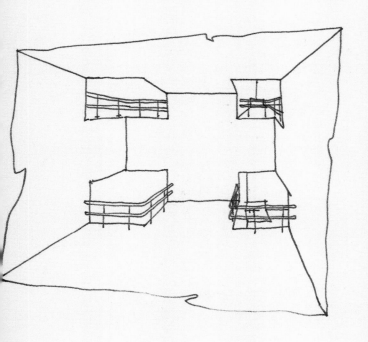

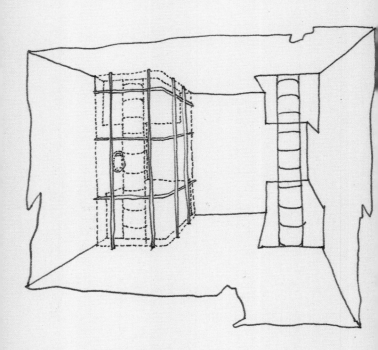

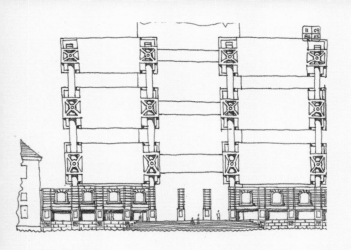

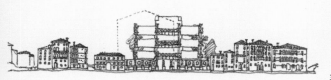

387

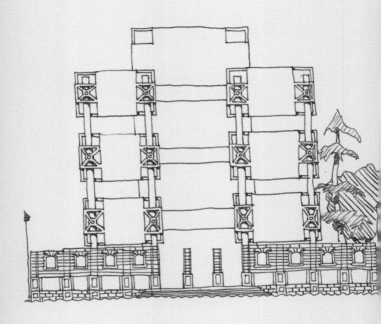

388

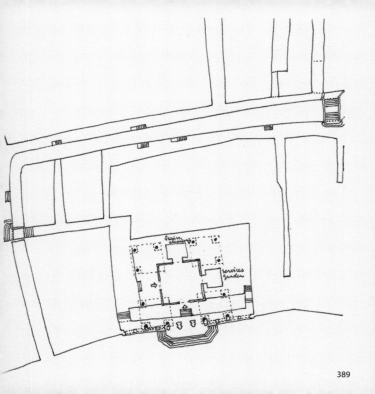

389

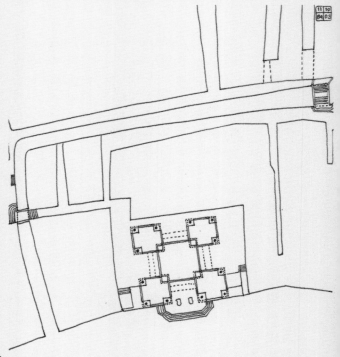

390

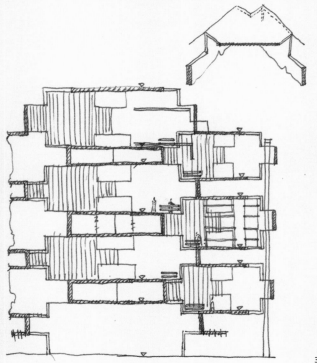

391

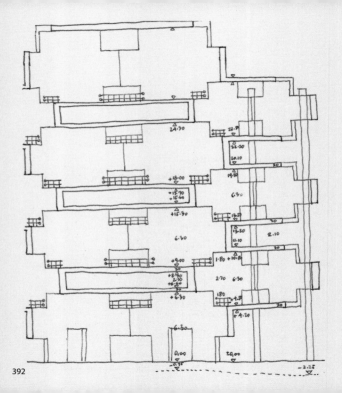

392

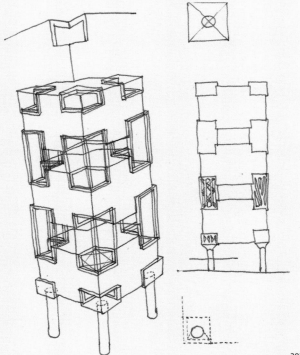

393

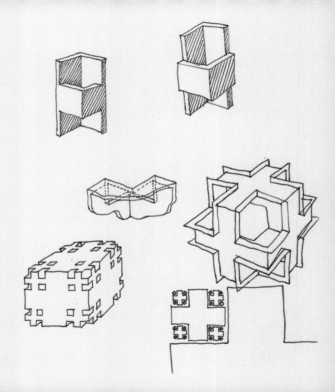

394

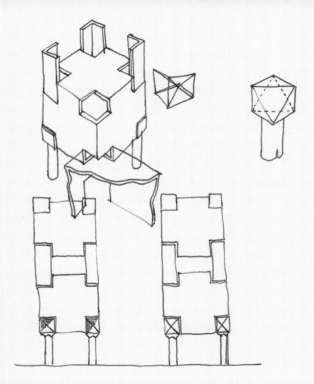

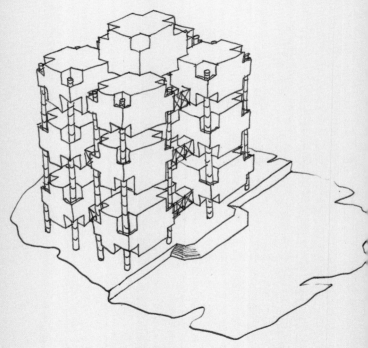

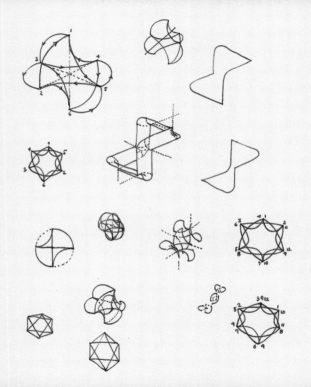

397

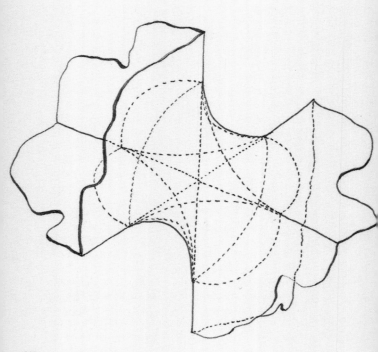

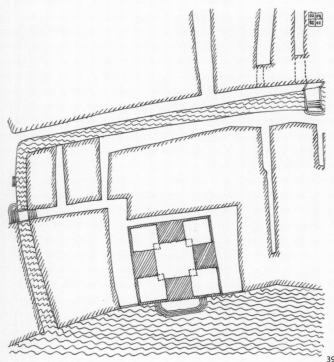

399

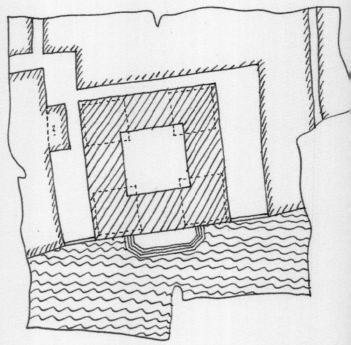

400

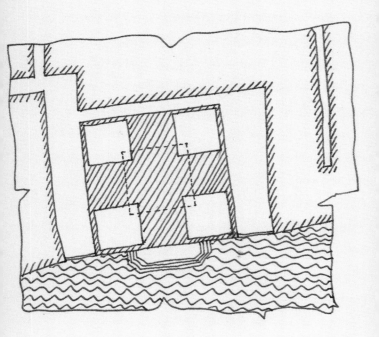

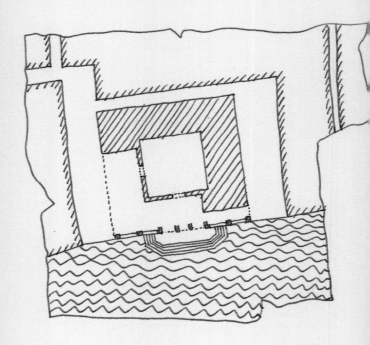

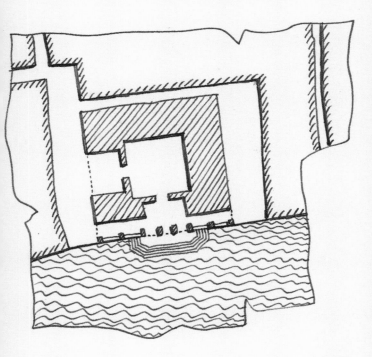

403

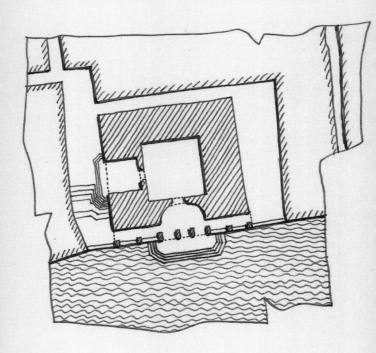

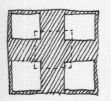

3.

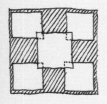

2.

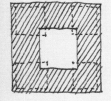

1.

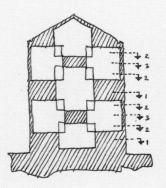

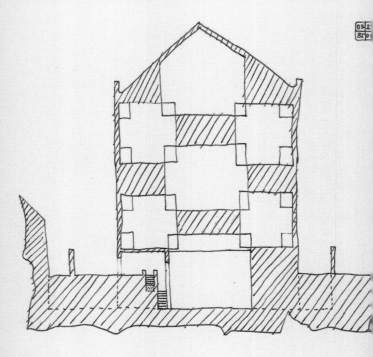

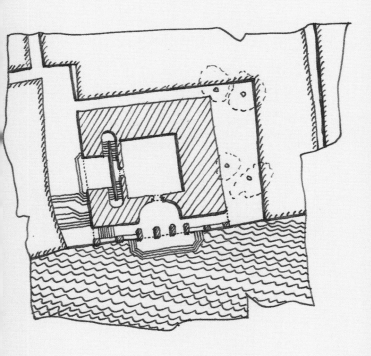

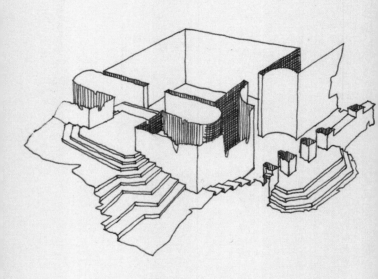

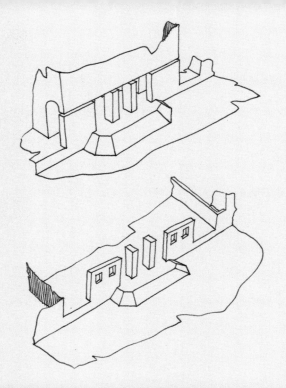

409

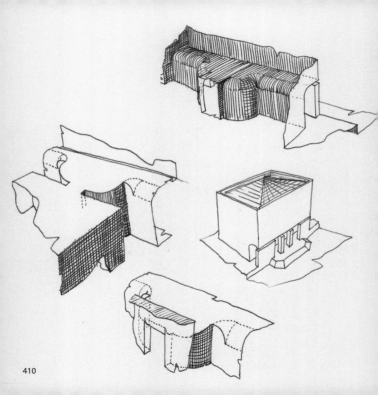

410

411

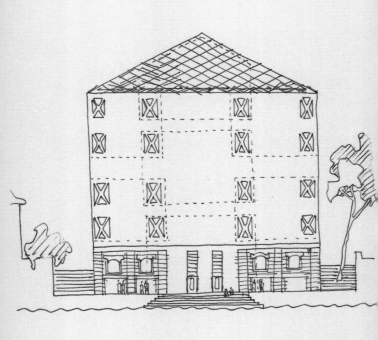

413

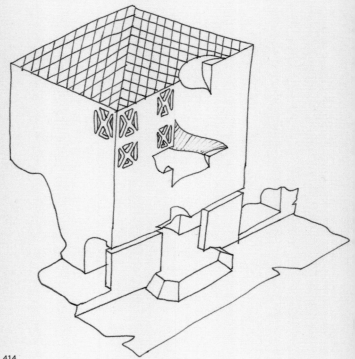

414

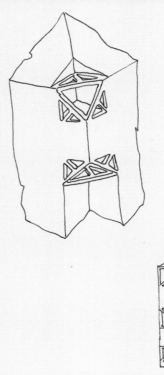

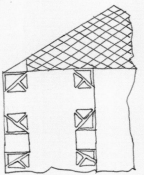

415

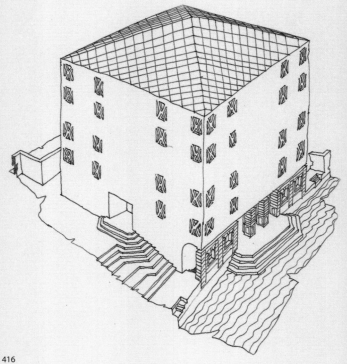

416

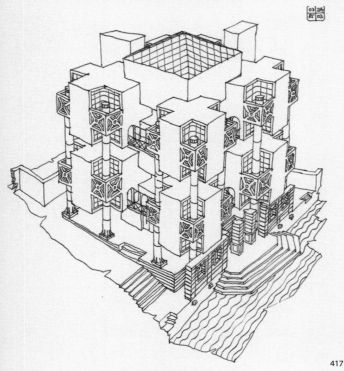

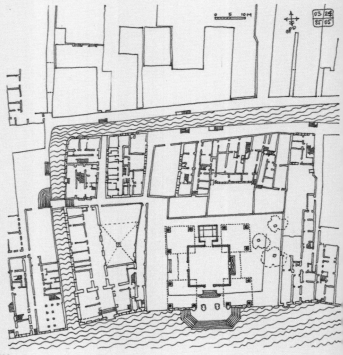

418

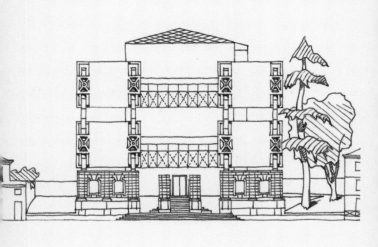

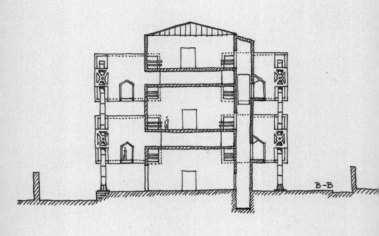

B-B

0   5   10M

420

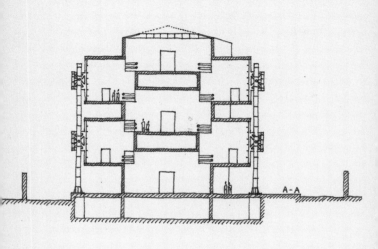

A - A

0   5   10M

421

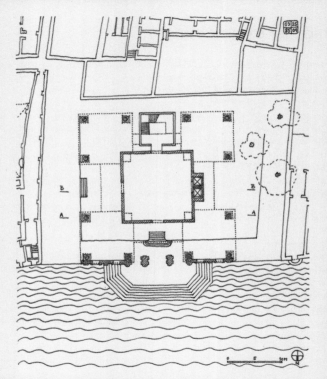

enice Gate Competition

On the following pages moments of an investigative process are depicted to test the validity d the feasibility of the drawings in the physical, perceptional, and poetic context. Physical and ilitarian considerations suggested an unorthodox solution to the parking and processing of the ses.

The compact arrangement of the ring produced not only a clear and uninterrupted flow of destrian circulation but it intends to "elevate" the act of arrival and departure to a magical and thical complexity. The (admittedly biased) perception of the designers was that the descending he buses through the tunnel to the ascending and rotating disc as an appropriate introduction the arrival to Venice. Displacement and momentary disorientation coupled with the spatially biguous inside-outside relation of the truncated cone (hopefully) prepare the surprise of being re. Rain (or perhaps an artificially recirculated waterfall from the roof) creates a curtain of water, eil to be pierced by the arriving or departing buses, a phenomenon memorable for people ide or outside of the bus.

A secret spot of the site revealed itself when the axes of the two ramp-wells and the axis of bridge over the Rio Nuovo intersected in the same point where the rectangular line pointed, ich was projected from the intersection of the diagonals on the office building site. This locus of site is the center of the third well: the turntable/elevator of the bus terminal. e (maybe subconscious) strategy of the design of the office/gate building followed similar pat- ns like the bus terminals: the goal has been to elevate mostly mundane functions to a morable mental image.

The prescribed functions are dully located in the two halves of the building, an exploration to create oneness in spite of physical separation. The typology of the Dogana del Mare served as well to articulate this Gate-Masque, which, at least for us, offers other enigmatic archaic reference. We proposed post-tensioned concrete pillars, steel roof structure in the bus terminal, in situ concrete by the other buildings with external-internal wall surfaces stuccoed with the exception of the gate, where marble inlay is proposed at certain locations. By proposing the use of Italian marble only as a veneer, but quarried from two large pieces in three-story heights in full width of the wedge, we intend to introduce nature in the grand moment of creation and to curb our human indulgence in the presence of such might.

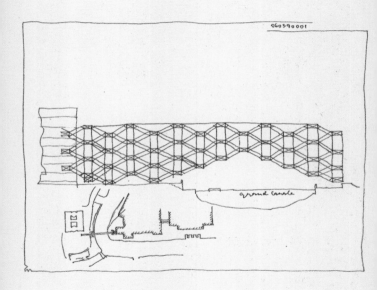

grand canale

426

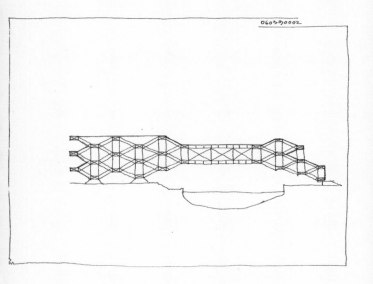

060390002

427

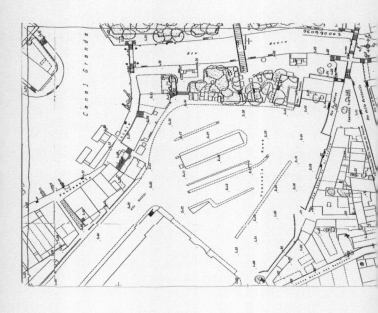

428

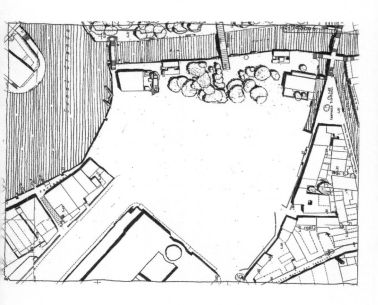

429

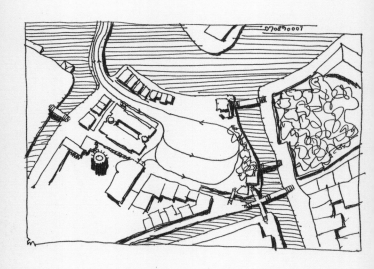

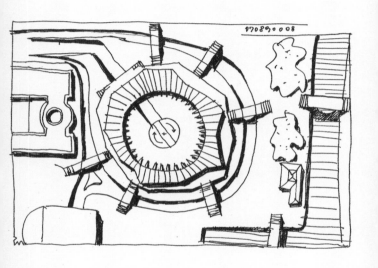

970890008

431

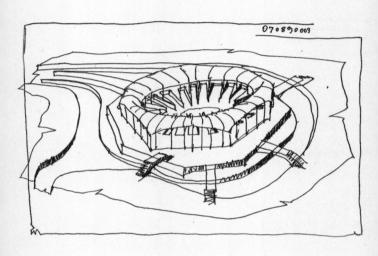

07089009

432

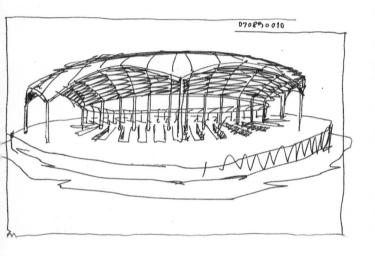

0708⬚0010

433

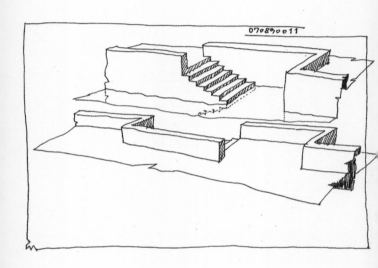

434

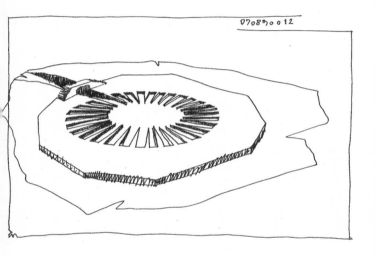

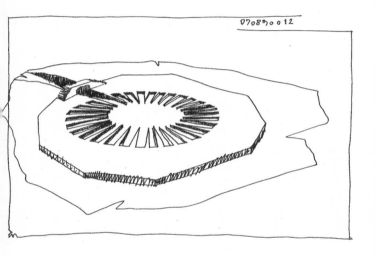

0708900012

435

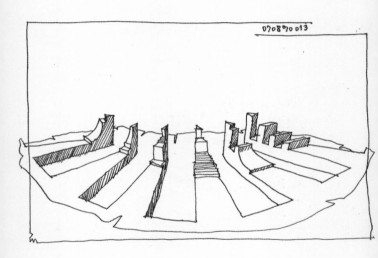

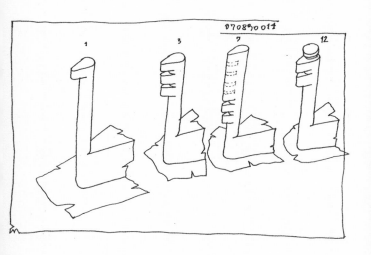

1   3   7   12

437

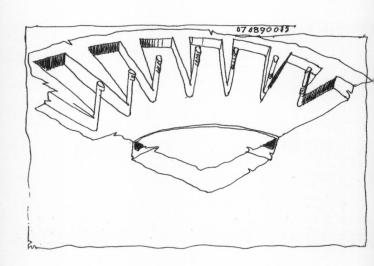

071890015

438

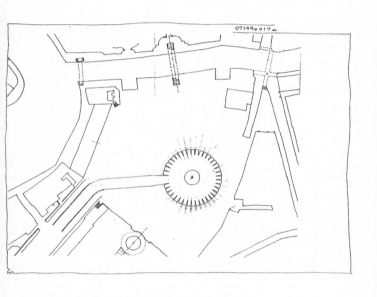

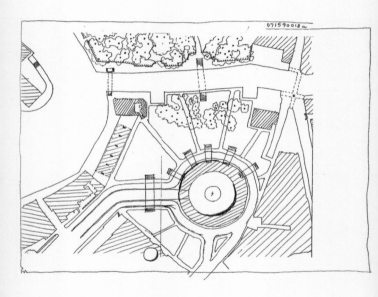

440

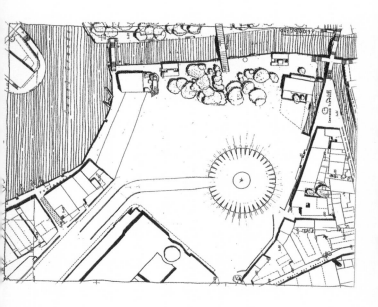

441

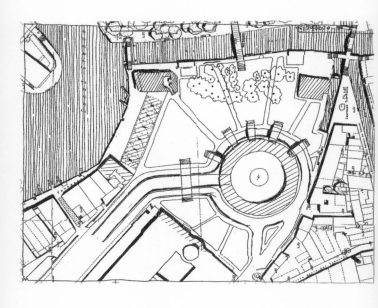

442

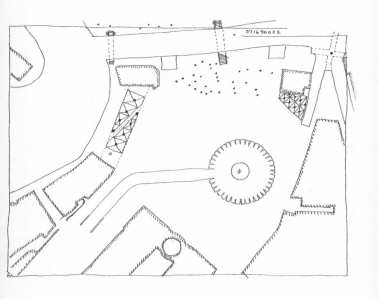

071690022

443

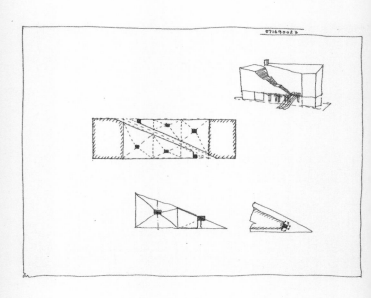

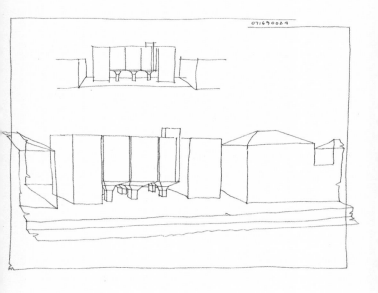

071690024

445

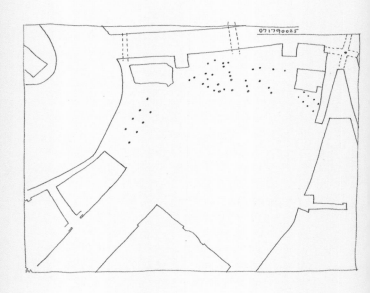

071790025

446

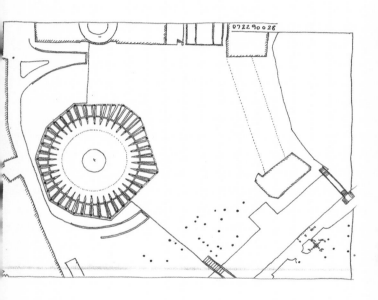

0722900028

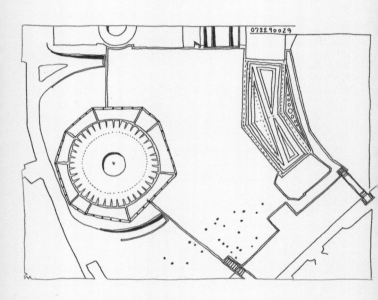

072290029

448

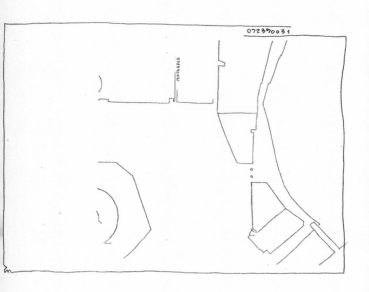

072390031

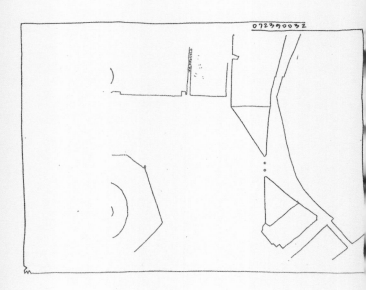

072390032

450

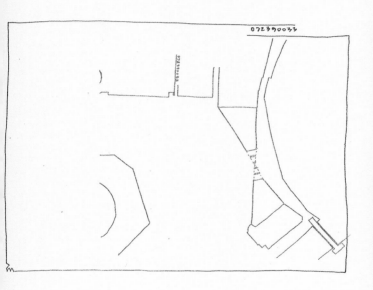

072390033

072390033

451

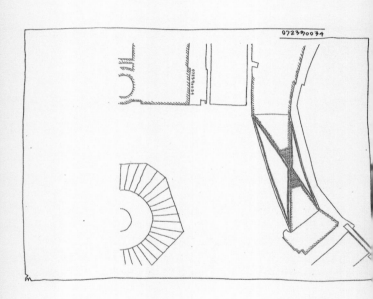

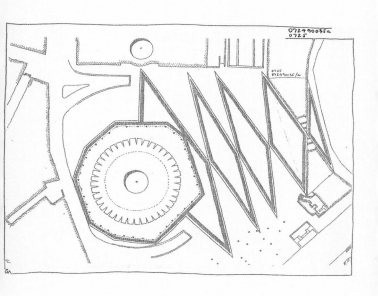

453

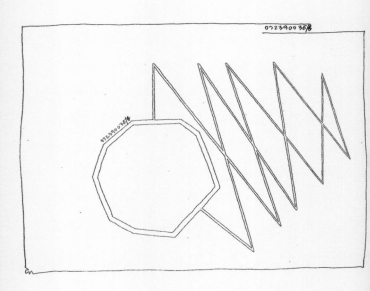

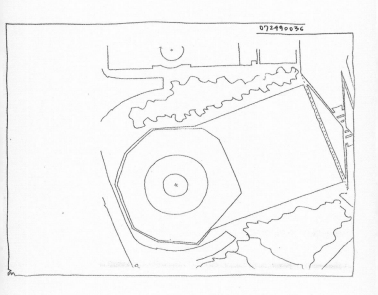

455

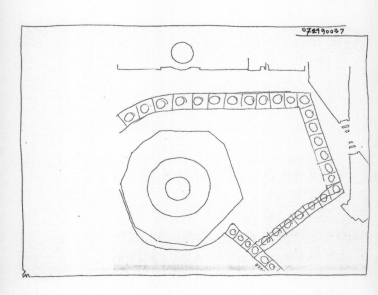

07290037

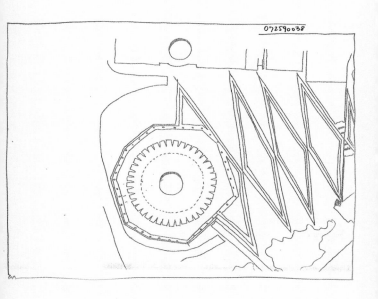

457

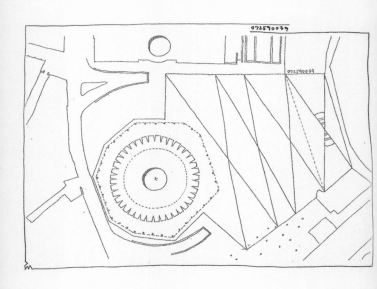

072590039

072590039

072590039

458

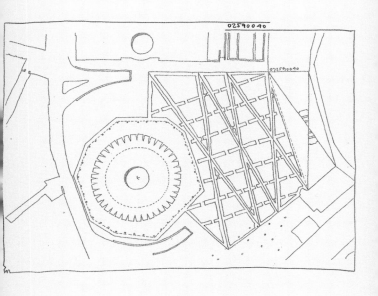

02590040

072590040

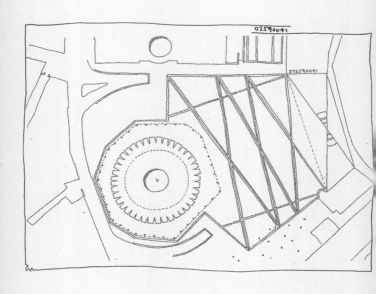

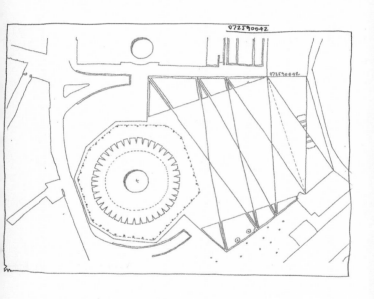

072590042

072590042

461

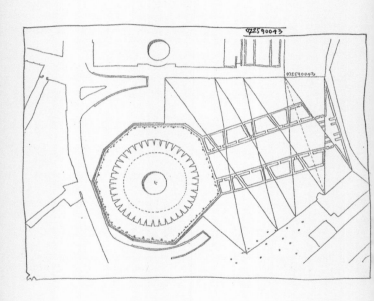

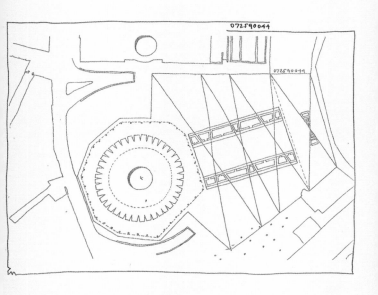

072590044

072590044

463

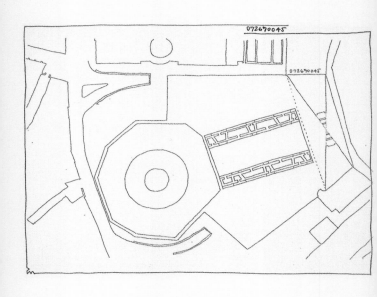

072670045

072670045

464

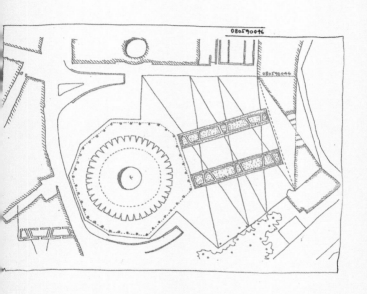

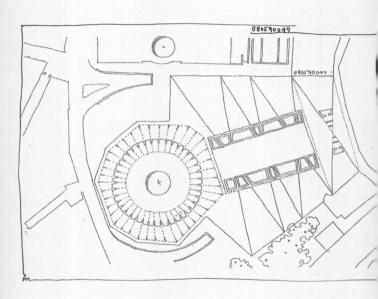

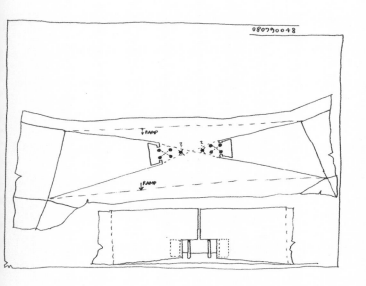

080790048

467

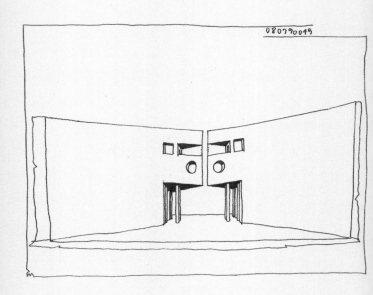

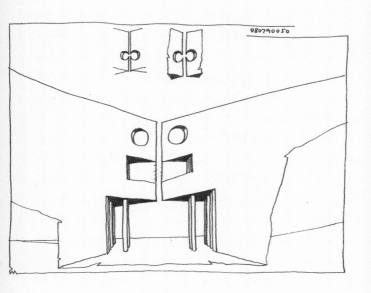

080790050

469

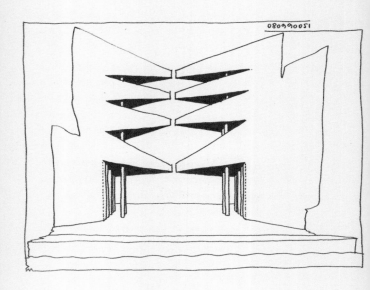

080990051

470

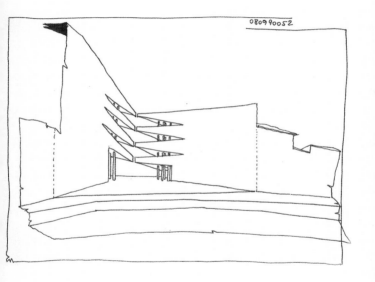

471

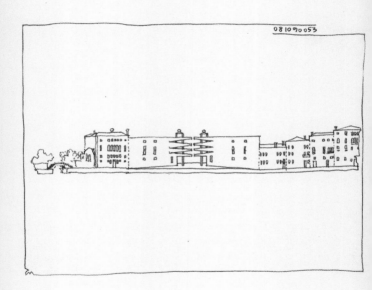

081090053

472

Treasures   Peter/Jordan

473

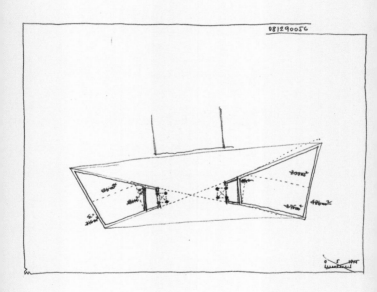

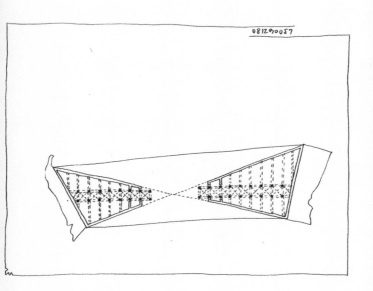

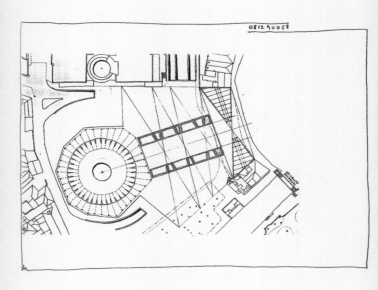

476

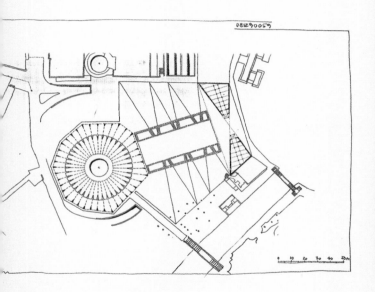

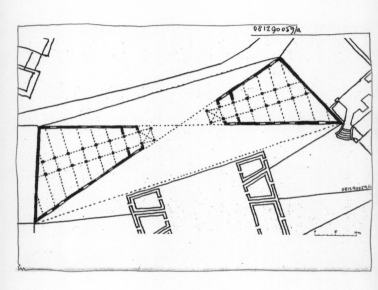

081290059/a

081290059/b

478

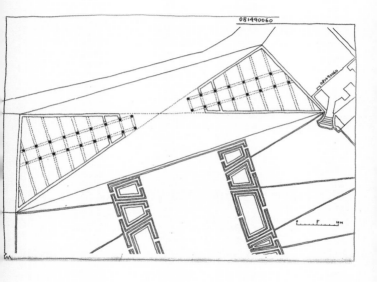

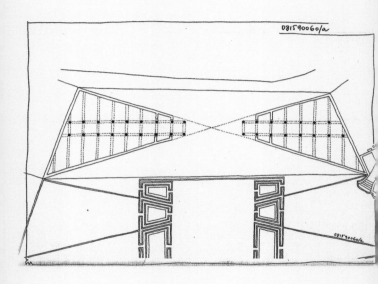

081590060/a

081590060/a

480

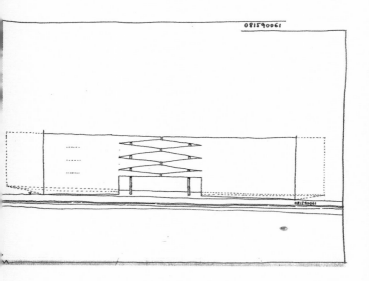

481

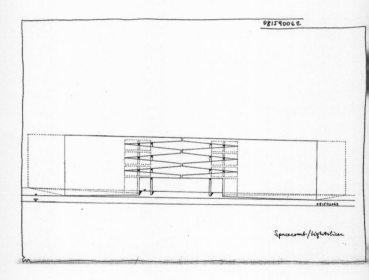

081590062

Spacecomb/lightslicer

482

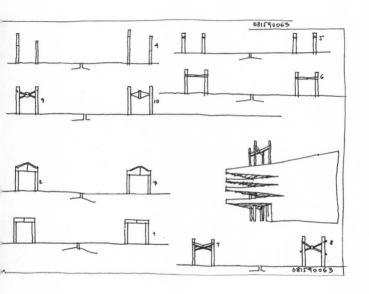

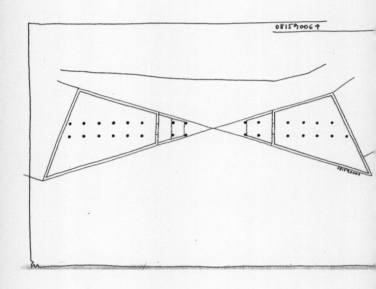

484

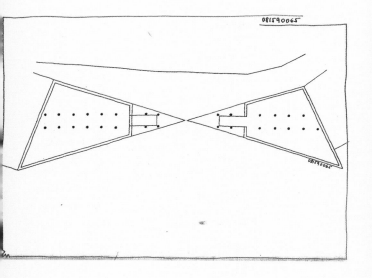

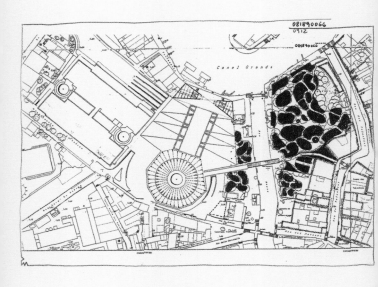

Canal Grande

081890066
0912

081890066

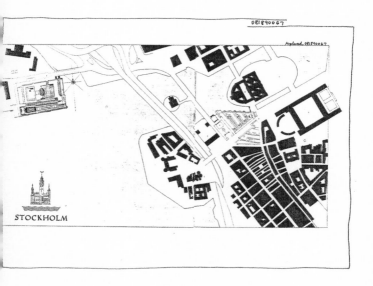

STOCKHOLM

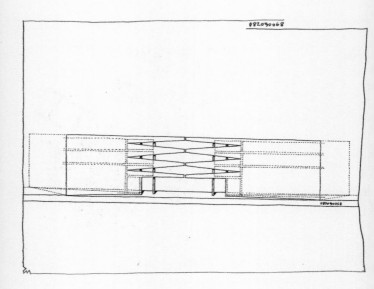

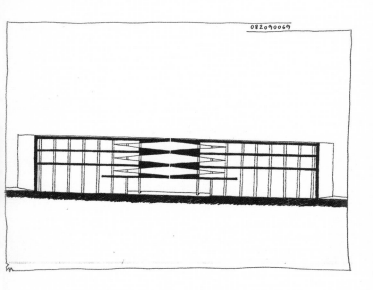

082090069

489

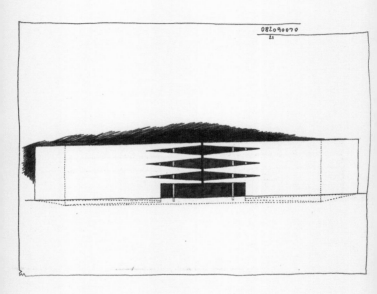

490

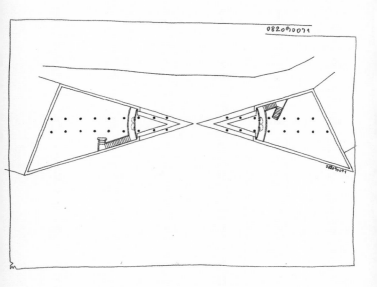

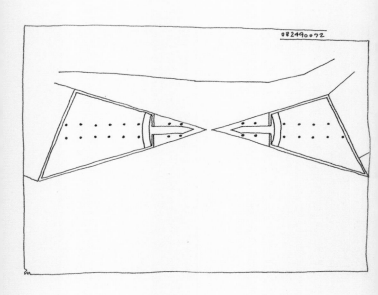

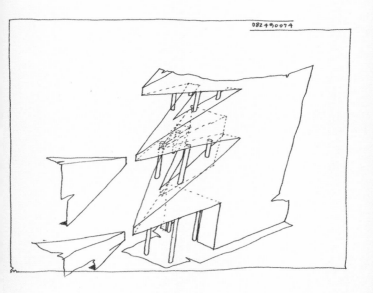

082490074

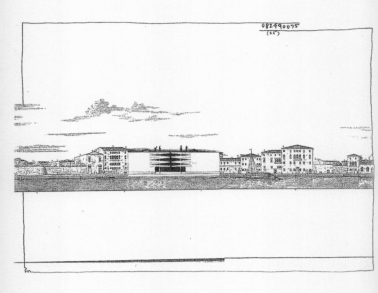

494

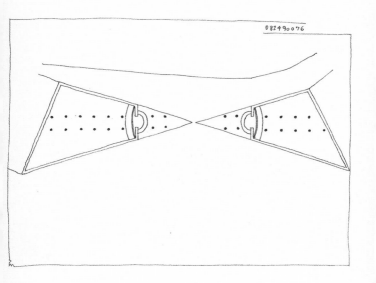

082490076

495

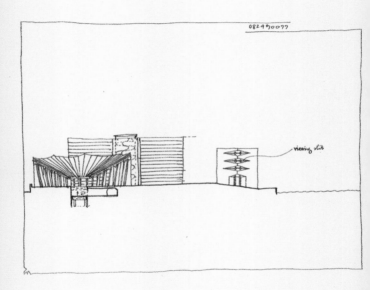

082490077

viewing slit

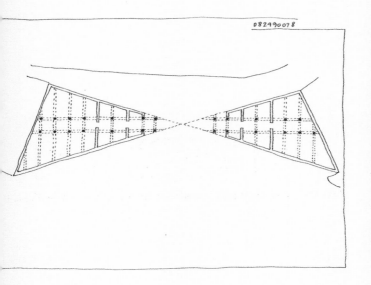

082490078

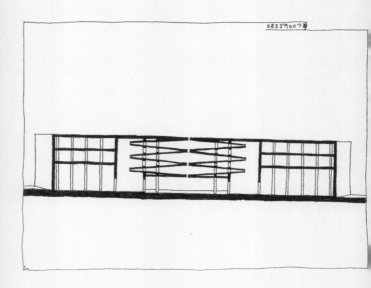

498

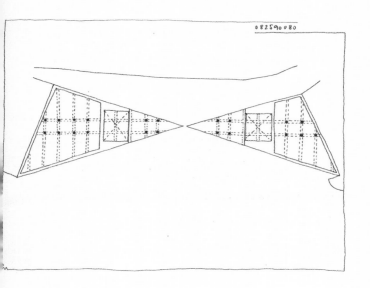

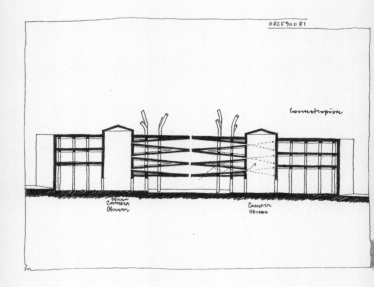

082590081

Cosmotropism

Obscura
Camera
Obscura

Camera
Obscura

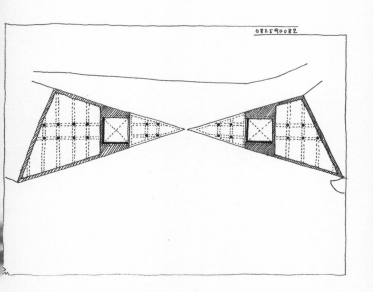

501

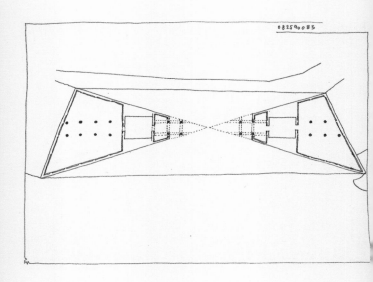

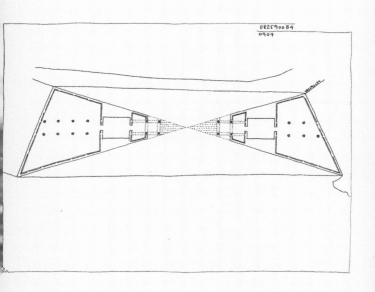

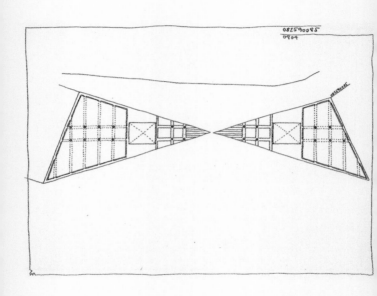

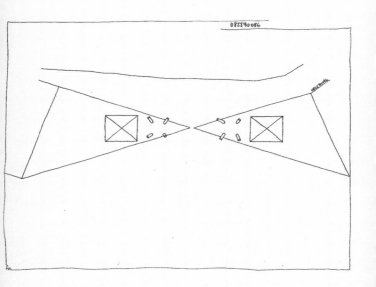

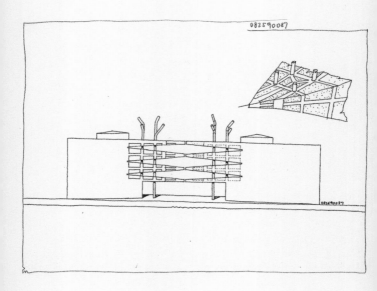

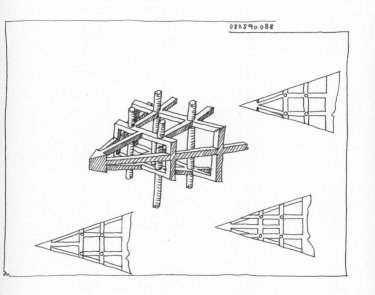

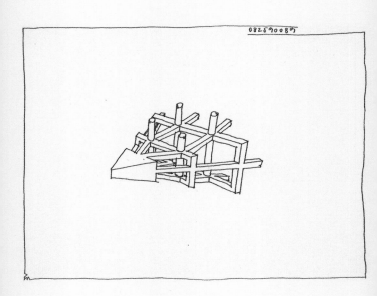

508

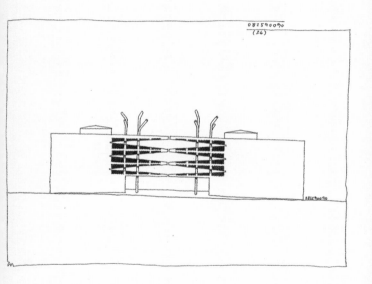

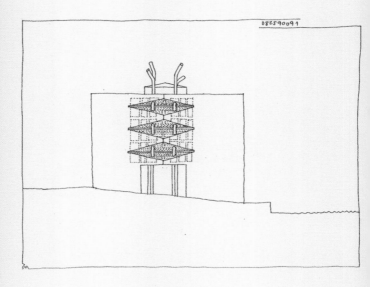

510

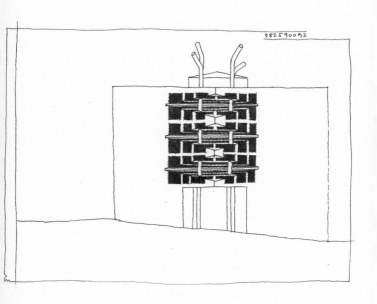

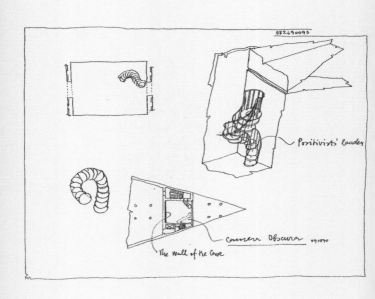

082690093

Positivists' leader

Camera Obscura 290890

The Wall of the Cave

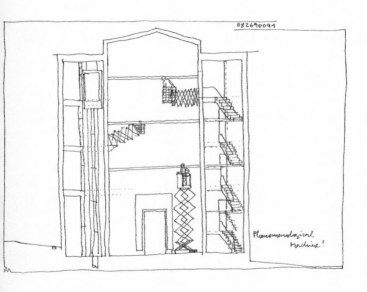

Phenomenological machine!

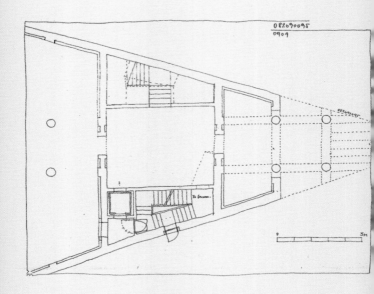

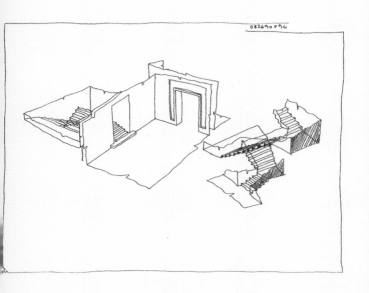

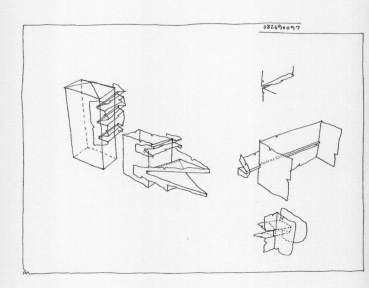

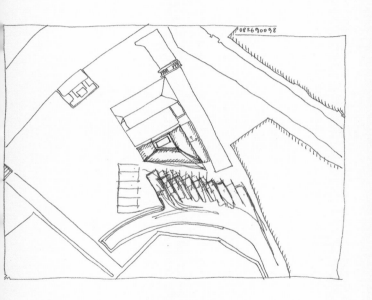

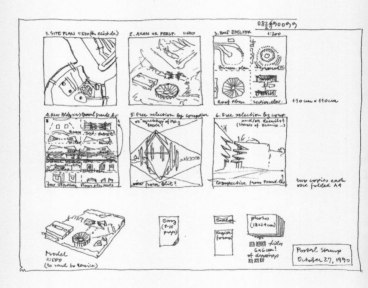

082690009g

1. SITE PLAN 1:500 (+ existch.) 2. AXON or PERSP. 1:500 3. BUS SHELTER 1:200

Bus stop plan   Roof plan / section, elev.   110 cm x 110 cm

4. New Bldg w/ general grade A1 5. Free selection by Composition or "morphology of the tower? 6. Free selection by comp. and/or details? (Stones of Venice ...)

view from slit?   Perspective from Pound Can?   two copies each one folded A4

Model 1:500 (to send to Venice)

Essay (8-10 pages)

Bracket / Registr. forms

photos (18×24 cm)

slides 6×6 cm? of drawings

Postal Stamp October 27, 1990

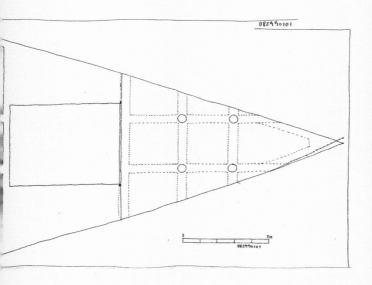

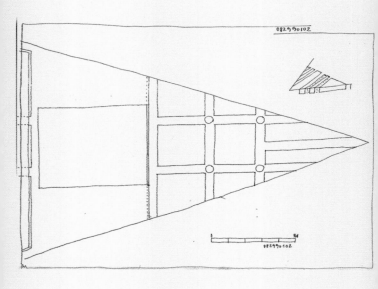

0829790102

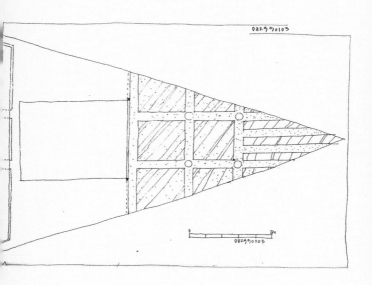

082970103

082970103

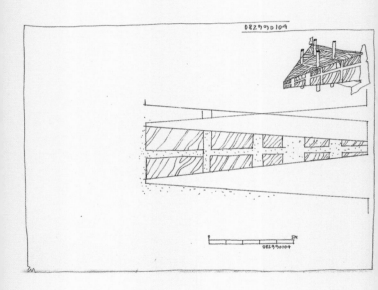

082990104

082990104

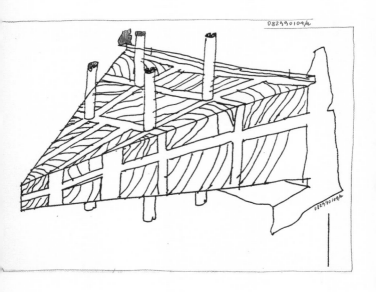

082890109/L

082890109/L

523

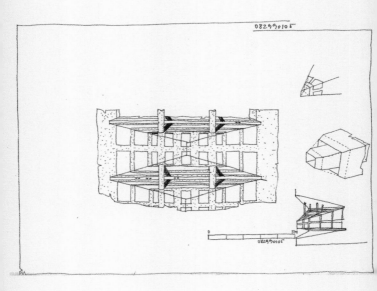

524

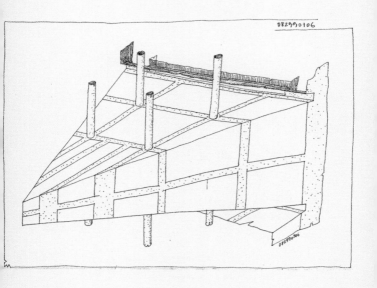

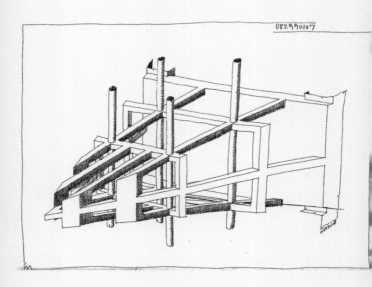

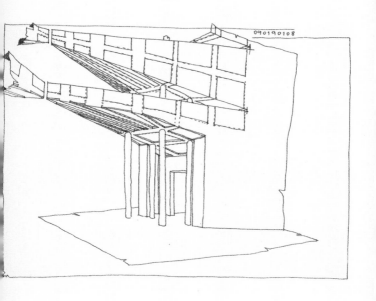

527

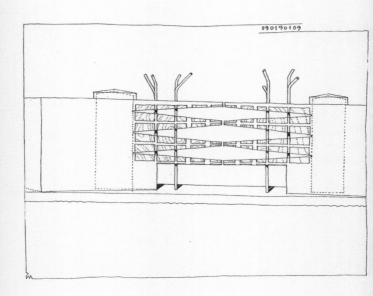

528

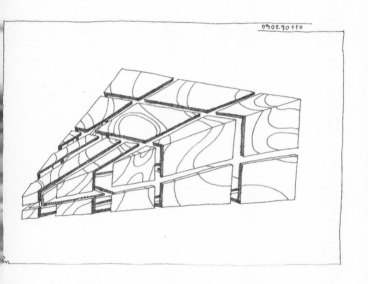

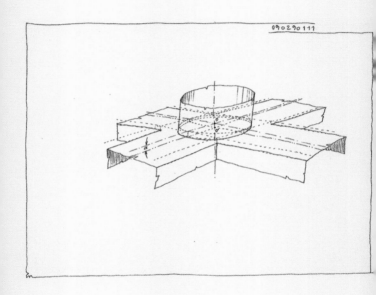

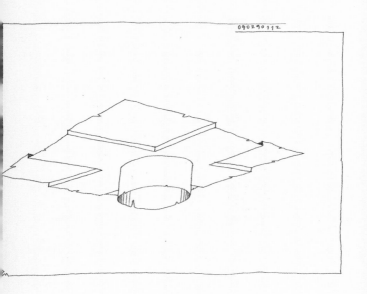

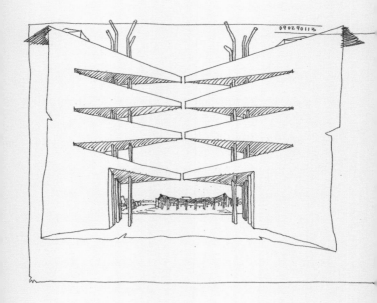

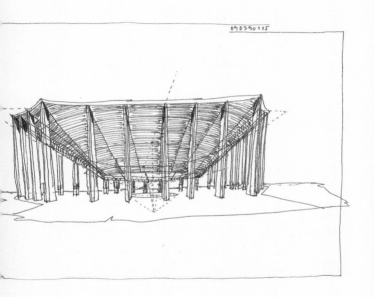

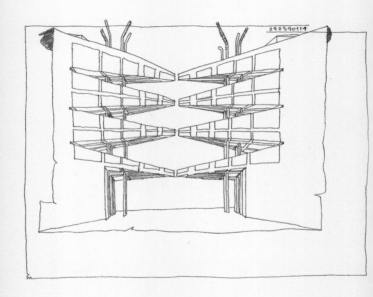

090390114

534

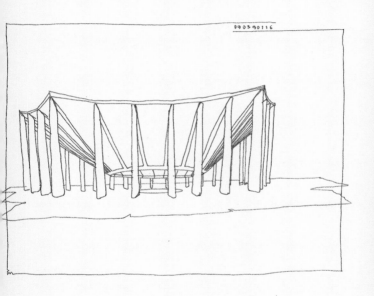

090390116

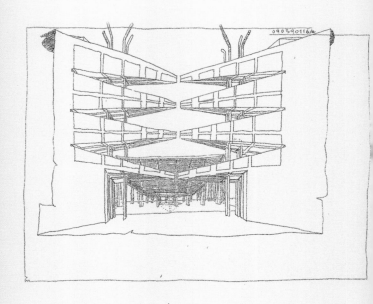

09059116/a

536

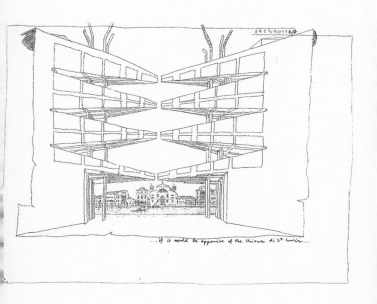

...if it would be opposite of the Chiesa di Ste Lucia...

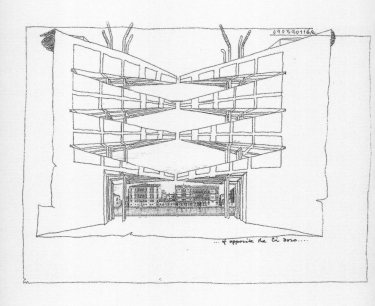

... if opposite the Ca' Doro ...

538

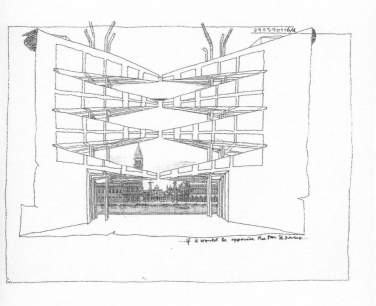

...if it would be opposite the Piazza San Marco...

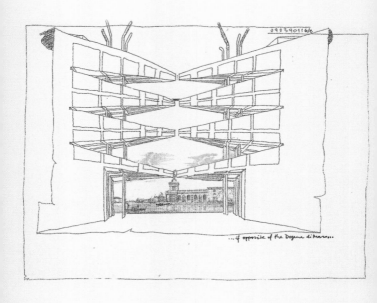

...if opposite of the Dogana di Mare...

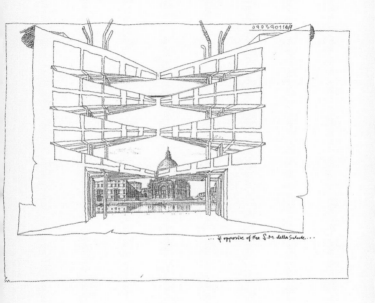

... if opposite of the S.M. della Salute ...

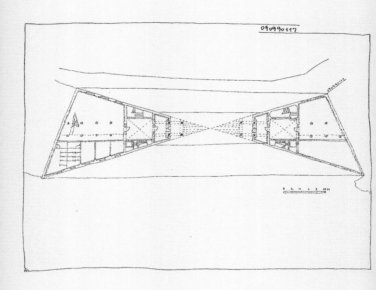

542

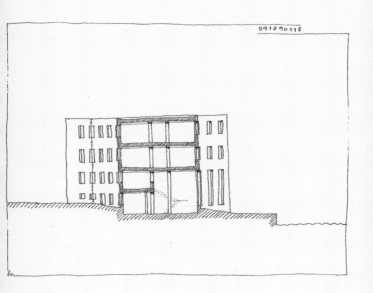

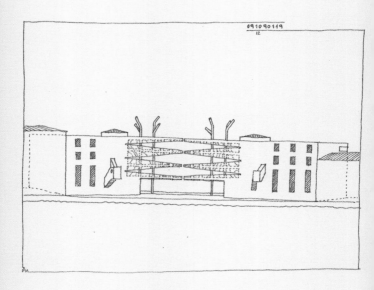

544

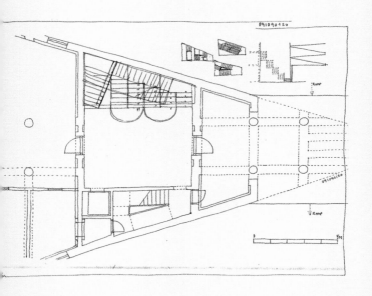

545

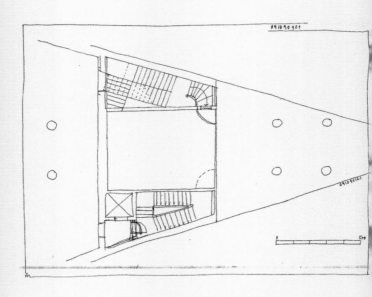

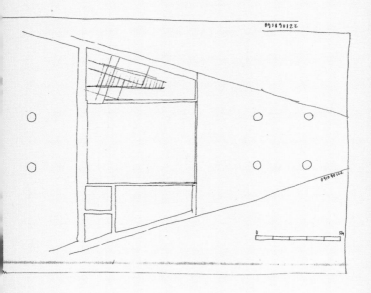

0918901122

0910901122

547

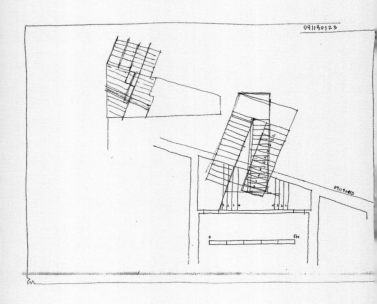

091190123

0911900123

548

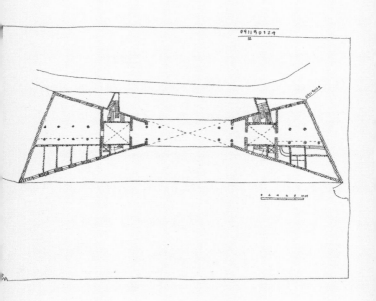

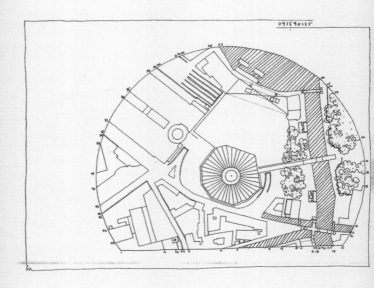

550

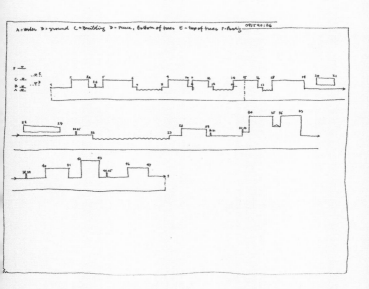

A = water   B = ground   C = Building   D = Fence, Bottom of trees   E = top of trees   F = sky   0915 90:26

551

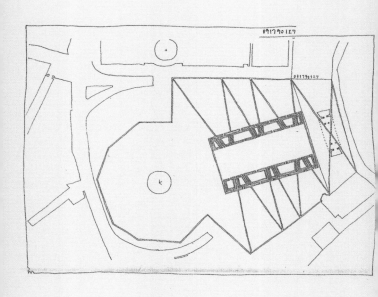

091790127

091790127

552

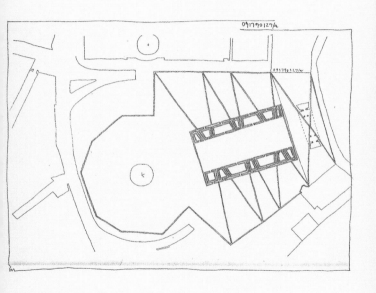

553

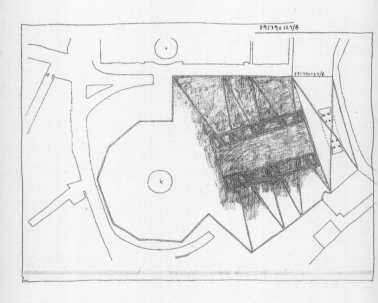

554

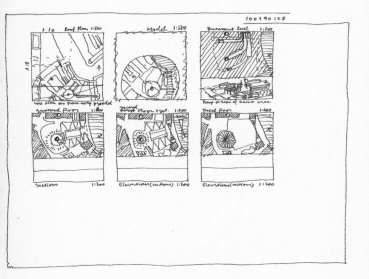

1.10   Roof Plan 1:500   Model 1:500   Basement level 1:200

A.10

site plan on space very provded   Persp vision of entire area

ground floor   1:200   second floor Plan typ. 1:200   third floor   1:200

Sections   1:200   Elevations (sections) 1:200   Elevations (sections) 1:200

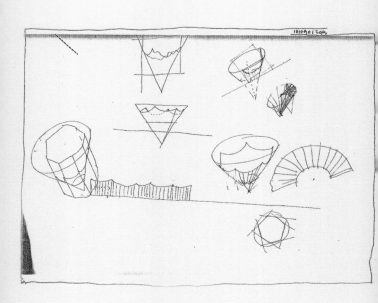

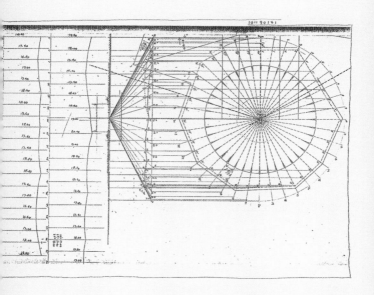

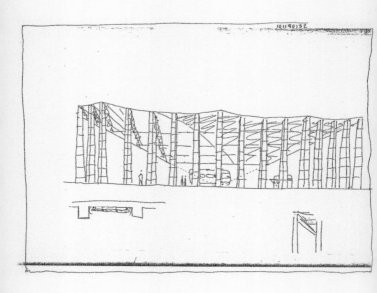

558

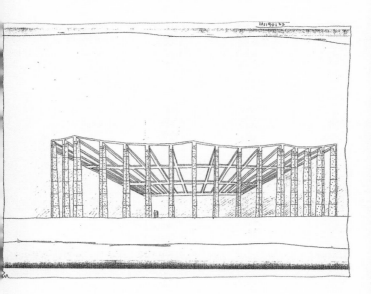

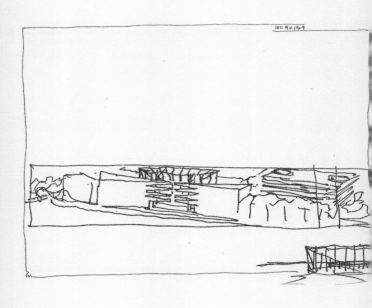

1011901304

560

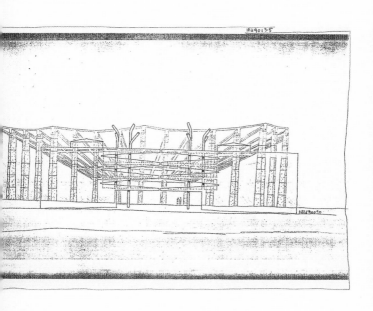

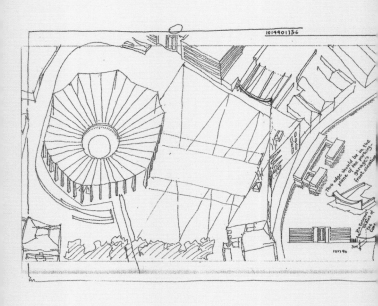

1014901136

This edge should be in the plane of the parapet + front dome

At extreme station

1013 96

3m

562

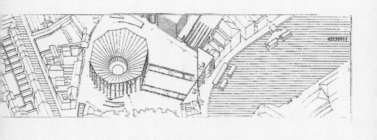

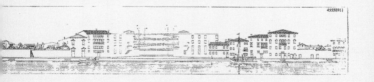

563

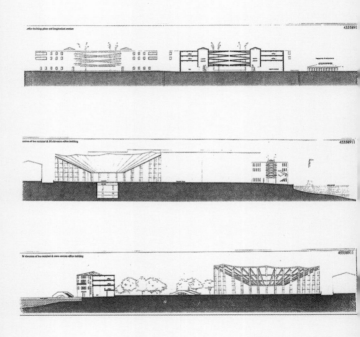

office building plans and longitudinal section   45558911

section of bus terminal & DS elevation office building   45558911

W elevation of bus terminal & cross section office building   45558911

564

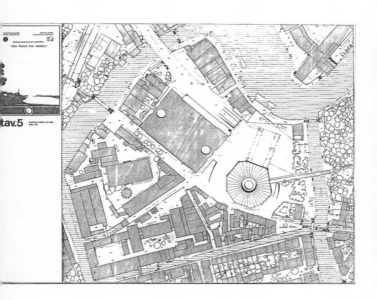

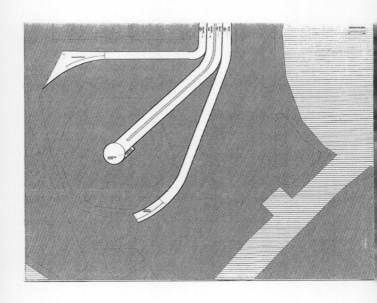

ground floor plan

567

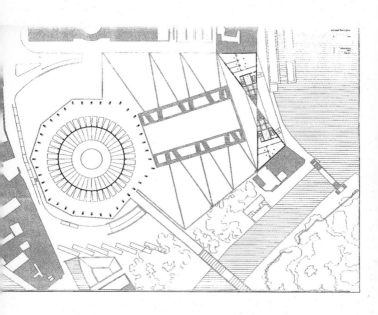

Drawing, Thinking, Making

Robert McCarter
Ruth and Norman Moore Professor of Architecture
Washington University in St. Louis

The drawings of Peter Magyar—his thinking with ink—are fundamentally concerned with the idea of space shaped for human habitation. Drawing is here understood as a way of sensing precisely the spatial skins enclosing the rooms in which we live. As a way of designing, it involves the active touching and shaping of the space of inhabitation, much as a potter shapes the clay to form a vessel. Frank Lloyd Wright, who defined the architect's primary task as the making of "the space within," placed large clay pots at strategic spatial joints within his home and studio, Taliesin West, where they serve to remind us of the nature of the vessel enclosing us. As Magyar points out, space is perceptible only through the boundaries that enclose it, the surfaces that shape our interior experience. As it was for Aldo van Eyck, the idea of the interior is here understood to include all the spaces shaped for human inhabitation – rooms, courtyards, plazas, streets, even the city as a whole.

"Drawings are the first physical embodiment of thought," Magyar states, and "therefore, no drawing should exist without this duality present: the ability to be realized, and the containment of thoughts." In other words, the hand drawing is the place where thinking and making are joined together. In a time when leading architectural academics have stated that those in the university should not be concerned with making, only with thinking—as if such a thing were even possible in architecture—Magyar's drawings stand for a fundamentally different approach to both education and practice. While increasingly rare in our digitally dominated schools and offices, hand drawing is made by engaging tactile thought, allowing both the body and the eye to participate in shaping the spaces of inhabitation. Hand drawing is also a slow and thoughtful process—a process which actively joins thinking and making—as Tod Williams and Billie Tsien have indicated, "Buildings are still constructed with hands, and it seems that the hand still knows best what the hand is capable of doing. As our hands move, we have the time to think and observe our actions."

In Magyar's words, the three projects for Venice presented here serve to illustrate "the excavation process of the organically-embedded idea as latently present in the site, context, culture and program, and [how the idea] is embodied by the physicality of the structure … [In this process] the major 'description' is written in the drawings." A number of principles may be discerned in this statement, starting with the idea that architecture is literally embedded in its site. Making space by carving and shaping heavy, anchored, earthbound masses, Magyar's particular genius is his ability to literally draw his buildings up out of their sites, through an organic fusion of geometry and ground. He intentionally limits himself to stereotomic, wall- based building, and this allows him to engage the local tradition of masonry construction of Venice. Magyar conceives of architecture as literally being built from the ground up, and his drawings represent this fundamental sense of anchorage to and embedment in the surface of the earth – the primary surface of our inhabitation. In this way of making, carving, or inscribing spaces into the surface of the earth, we are close to Adrian Stokes's belief that architectural space comes from carving as the construction that reveals a space and shape latent in the material or place, as opposed to modeling as the creation of a form that is imposed on the material or place.

Magyar's designs invariably exhibit the greatest respect for the existing urban forms of the city, and he complements this contextualism by imbuing his buildings with a hint of anthropo-morphic character. His designs are part of a central European engagement of the historical and physical thickness of the city, an engagement of articulate wall surfaces that, as Anthony Alofsin h

scribed it, allows the buildings to "speak" of the place and culture. Magyar's building designs, as
engagements of the fabric of the thick urban wall, are not only embedded in their place, Venice,
but in the history of architecture. His work is part of a living tradition, which includes historical
figures such as Joze Plecnik, Jan Kotera, Josef Gocar, Bela Lajta, Aladar Arkay, and Otto Wagner,
the early work of the Tendenza, and the contemporary works of Heinz Tesar and Raimund Abraham.
Those that are part of this tradition of urban architecture refuse to allow historical form, stereotomic mass-walls, and the ancient geometric structure of architecture to become disengaged
from either their physical or disciplinary place, losing their gravitas and floating as pure referential
form – the characteristics of historicist post-modernism which have so devalued our disciplinary
heritage.

On the other hand, the work of the living tradition, of which Magyar is a part, reminds us of
what we have lost in our insistence on a never-ending avant-gardism in architecture, wherein the
baby of disciplinary history was thrown out with the dirty bath water of historicist post-modernism.
This drawings, Magyar places primary emphasis on the making of "the space within" for inhabitation; on the spaces and walls of the city, following Aldo Rossi's *L'Architettura della Citta*; and
the forthright engagement of historical form, following Louis Kahn's understanding that, for the
architect, "history is a friend."

In his work in historical places and within the history of the discipline, Magyar states, "the
comprehensive and operative application of the values of the past is called upon to assist in the
invention of the future." In an indication of his distance from the current "masters of emptiness" in
architecture (as George Steiner has called the post-modernists—both historicist and avant-gardist),
Magyar holds that architecture is concerned first and foremost with love and responsibility, and
that architecture's "ethical measure is social usefulness" – in other words, that architecture's task is
to edify. In this, Magyar is quite close to Gianni Vattimo, who states, "Edification has two principal

meanings – to build and to be morally uplifting … That is, edification must be ethical, entailing communication of value choices.

In the present situation … the only possibility of edifying in the sense of building is to edify in the sense of 'rendering ethical,' that is, to encourage an ethical life: to work with the recollection traditions, with the traces of the past, with the expectations of meaning for the future."

Magyar pursues a timeless—not timely—way of building, and he understands that the experience of the inhabitants is the only valid method of evaluating architecture. Magyar's designs aspire to something permanent and lasting, and in this they admirably embody Louis Kahn's visionary definition: always more than the sum of its measurable aspects—the practical, a work of architecture is that which allows us to experience the immeasurable—the poetic.

Introduction for Urban Innuendoes

Kendra Schank Smith
Ryerson University

The drawings in Peter Magyar's newest book, *Urban Innuendoes*, are remarkably reflective. They comprise an elegant combination of past and future. As inspired archeology, they represent a conversation between creative innovation and drawings that appear fractured and incomplete. In this way, the memories of the drawer inspire the invention. We are reminded of thoughts by Wolfgang Meisenheimer in *Daidalos 25*, when he writes about poetic drawings that try to depict the indefinable. They are "traces of the memory and the dreams of the drawer, outbreaks of temperament and wit, provocation of the observer, riddles, vague evocations or gestures of philosophical thesis … The transferals and interpretations which result from them move on all possible levels." Most importantly, Dr. Magyar's drawings cause the viewer to participate; to engage the questions they ask, and to continually contemplate their meaning. This is the power of drawings in that they

n be insightful, contemplative, profound, playful, and serious, all at the same time. The levels
understanding can represent past, present, and future, but also question architectural space,
lume, and context woven into aspirations and potentialities. The ability of these drawings by Dr.
ngyar to "move on all possible levels" is their strength.

The assured and controlled lines of these drawings describe thoughtful urban interventions.
oking to future environments, the drawings are parturient in that they hold potentialities. Partu-
nt suggests bringing forth or giving birth to something. The word evokes both the anticipation
a birth and production of something such as an idea or discovery. In *Urban Innuendoes*, each
awing provokes expectations of a unique solution to a question of urban context. These draw-
s can be both universal, giving us suggestions of ways to think about context common to all cit-
, and, at the same time, can specifically address design for the future. The speculative buildings
ovoke contemporary solutions to design issues. To "bring forth" relies on something exciting just
low the surface, evoking the emergence of the bold and new. Anticipation of the thing about to
born is fraught with ambiguity, but a certain amount of vagueness is not to be avoided.
tually, the ambiguity of these drawings encourages the observer to ponder. To ponder is to
tively engage in imagination and contemplation. As a play on words, these drawings call upon us
ponder the profound.

The human mind will always attempt to find order out of chaos and it is this activity that
ovokes the viewer to look longer – to revel in the possibilities. As viewers, we cannot passively
serve, we are compelled to actively associate and speculate. The drawings cause a certain willed
ulity.

By actively engaging their speculative narrative, they bring the observer to "see" the future.
e seeing is not a realistic view but rather a view with greater depth, a view that requires effort
d imagination.

Dr. Magyar's drawings are not chaotic, they are instead engaging. The lines both contemplative and quick (containing wit) encourage consideration. With the process of meditation, associations will ruminate and new notions can transpire. Again, to transpire questions the emergence of new ideas, and parturient potential.

This is not all speculation, as the lines act as the narrative. Drawn in sepia ink, the marks on the paper show a degree of transparency in some places and the denseness of hesitation in other. All the drawings use one type of pen, and one line weight, which indicates an evenness of tone. Although the consistency forces the viewer to question the emphasis of one element over another, this is the beauty of the drawings in that they give credibility to the whole. The even treatment places the designs perfectly within their context since the buildings are considered part of their site even before they are built.

Again, we are reminded of archeology, as the broken edges provide the opportunities to look underneath, behind, and around. This is where the drawings satisfy on many levels, they provide questions and solutions at the same time. The lines tell the story; they effectively frame the narrative and consequently become "thinking lines." As a result, this is where analysis and speculation meet, the place where the pondering of the past touches the design solution. Parturient also evokes connotations of labor. The labor in Dr. Magyar's drawing is not a labor of toil, but rather a labor of commitment: to "dig" deeply into his memory, his psyche, to provide the foundation for anticipation of architectural expression.

Grace McGarvie wrote, "an architect is the drawer of dreams." By dreams we can expect that she meant the dreams of our sleep, but also the aspirations of our responsibilities as architects. To envision the future is no small task, as it is bound up with memory, imagination, and fantasy. The reader will not be able to draw easy conclusions about the drawings in this book, but will be compelled to return to the questions that are raised in the projects. Peter Magyar's drawings, so

utifully reproduced in Urban Innuendoes, are the diagrams of these narratives, both of memo-
and speculation. They are part of the act of bringing architecture to life.

omething Almost Being Said

er Magyar

Due to my long professional participation, I list only the major aspects of my activities. I have
ned, taught, researched, and practiced on four of the five continents, and directed two and
nded one schools of architecture at American universities. I wrote a series of six books: the *Pen
Diaries*. I mention them here because the title is recent, but its esoteric relevance was always
ortant to me.

Among my works are three competitions for the Hungarian National Theater, one opera
se in Paris and one in Taiwan, a museum beside the Pyramids of Giza and for one in Venice, an
rnational port in Japan, theaters from Nigeria to Cardiff, libraries in Stockholm and Alexandria,
ddition to the Prado in Madrid, and a memorial for Nelson Mandela in Cape Town, South Africa.
se are only a few of the more than hundred projects I designed. With Dr. Antal Lazar, we just
lished *Making Evergreen Architecture*, which contains hundreds of process drawings. We ex-
nged them by fax between Pennsylvania and Budapest as we designed the sports and cultural
ter to the Hungarian capital. The complex opened with a fairy tale operetta on the last day of
4. My other built and unbuilt works are maybe less newsworthy, but filled my life with joy;
y provided irreplaceable sources of learning. Many of them served as lessons for continued
cation, like the houses for Gunnar Asplund, Michelangelo and Johann Sebastian Bach.

I borrowed the title of this account from the Bach recording by the internationally-renowned
nist Simone Dinnerstein: Something Almost Being Said. As in ancient religions the name of god

is forbidden to be pronounced by mortals, so in our art this undefinable secret is also the mystery – the ephemeral aim and context of the work. We have to know that we are only the messengers these secrets, and the work, if it is elevated enough, is never completely decipherable. Because of this uncertainty, only now did I have the courage to write down my *Arts Poetica*:

Working at the boundaries of the known, the unknown, and the unknowable, I prioritize the tw latter notions, and intend to excavate the preconscious from the subconscious strata. My tools are my pen, and lately the stylus (for drawing on digital tablets). The material starting point is the epidermis of the place, but from there one has to ascend to the rarefied spheres of thoughts and feelings. This float in the domains of the unknown and unknowable, unfortunately, during the design process and as the straight consequence of the same, shifts more and more towards the domain of the known and in the constructed reality, every unknown must be excluded. My process drawings aim to serve the prolon-gation of the floating phase, and interrogate that hope, whether the materialized reality could convey anything at all from the Icarusean gift, provided by the design-experience for its enthusiastic laborer.

The *Ars Poetica* ends here. I have to confess, however, that not all of my intents, as describe above, were accomplished. Among my drawings, it was almost impossible to find preconscious of subconscious ones. Obviously, the activity of drawing is a highly conscious action, but governed also by the previously mentioned regions of our psyche. Design is a mentally and corporally expe-rienced process, which step by step evokes the mythology of the building, applying the genetic memory of our physical body. Accordingly, architecture, through drawings, or, in fortuitous cases constructed form, realizes and embodies a philosophy provided it investigates the basic question of knowledge, reality, and existence. These are exactly the notions with which the *Oxford English Dictionary* defines philosophy. Living according to the "nulla dies sine linea" (no day without a line have drawn and archived around 10,000 drawings. One tenth of them are published in my books

Related to books, for a long time I worked on another project, an architectural fairy tale children. Only the title, *Spatial Fable* and the first paragraph exist: "and he began to write the drawing. Thoughts condensed to lines. 'Time will stop if you do this every day,' promised his her. So he wrote and wrote; houses for lords and emperors, barbers and professors, for people ifferent empires and dominions – sometimes only for himself. He discovered the world outside, even more, the secrets of his soul."

I intend to pursue answers to very simple questions related to architectural design, and, e importantly, the generation of ideas in architectural design.

Unlike in science, where an idea can be tested and the same method produces the same re- s, in our profession we expect that using the same inquiry methods we can arrive at completely erent results. Related to the what question, the object and the intent of our activity, I posit three ons: connotive, cognitive, and volitive (related to feeling, thinking, and will). My intent is, there- , to unify feeling and thinking through will. The will is manifested with drawing.

To answer the how question, I conduct my investigations with surface drawings and ceprints. In this intentionally simplified quest, the why question's answer is: this method ultaneously investigates, analyzes, explores, and articulates solid and void, matter and space. se spaceprints are, therefore, the first manifestations of the intended physical reality, so they are strating the transition of spirit to matter.

Architecture is about love, about giving, about service and responsibility. It deals with erent degrees of ritualization of the public and private domains, explores, discovers, applies, and brates the ideal and circumstantial conditions of sites, programs, cultures, and technologies. Its cal measure is social usefulness.

Dr. Thomas Kuhn in his book *The Structure of Scientific Revolutions* defines paradigms as "some accepted examples of actual scientific practice, which include laws, theory, application and instrumentalization. They should be sufficiently unprecedented and sufficiently open-ended." Architecture as a discipline seems to contain these two characteristics, since most of our building are supposed to be sufficiently unprecedented, and the design process sufficiently open-ended. He obviously failed to mention architecture among the sciences, but had he done so would have categorized our field as one in the pre-paradigm stage – like psychology in its early days when Dr. Sigmund Freud and Dr. Karl Jung established their respective theories based upon detailed analysis of self-observation. These observations were descriptive and interpretive but not yet normative. This non-normative status of our discipline will hopefully prevail, since the immeasurable aspects of our built environment are the ones that elicit wonder and awe, while the quantifiable is anticipated and only noticed in its absence and incorrect presence (such as wrong size or temperature). We might not be far from the truth if we use exactly the absence or presence of the immeasurable, as distinctive qualifier between building and architecture. Architects should aspire to go beyond the perfection and comfort of a building, and must attain the ability to produce "Architecture"; to refine and invent the best of the present and weigh its value in the future. The present, however, seems to be an extremely illusory concept, it transmutes itself as we speak into past. So the comprehensive and operative applications of the values of the past are called upon to assist in the invention of the future. We have to obtain the competent ability to include the measurable requirements into the newly modified environment, but transcend and coagulate them to the intangible magic of architecture. We believe that architecture is the highest manifestation of public art, channeled through the sensitive creativity of educated individuals. It unites the spatial and temporal aspects of art and affects one simultaneously in the visceral, cerebral, and cosmic dimensions.

Sustainable environment can be created only by a sustained design process with suspended judgment. The aim is to select and develop sustainable ideas. These ideas have to be able to more into physical systems, which will gradually grow to the intended architecture thanks to the critical

luation of the members of the design team. Since the sustained design process contains—
stly subconscious—influences from socio-cultural, technological, and climatic domains, with
help of targeted intuition, one can reconnect with the infinite source of traditional wisdom
he human race while simultaneously applying the latest achievements in the field of building
hnology.

To aspire to the highest art of craft by learning the craft of art, this sentence could be our
tto. If we scrutinize the role of craft in the present day construction industry, a very sad result
pears in comparison with the past. Our method of exhaustive and simultaneous exploration and
iculation in both the micro-geometrical and macro-geometrical scales through freehand draw-
s, testing the results in 3D models (both physical and virtual), and eventual application of the
est in the building information modeling system could only produce a contemporary realization
our aspirations. This somewhat immodest statement could become reality. With this applied and
d method, even the professional representatives of the client could have an almost real-time
ight during the conceptual design due to the recorded phase-drawings displayed on the Inter-
t. Drawings are the first physical embodiments of thoughts, therefore, no drawing should exist
hout this duality present: the ability to be realized and the containment of thoughts. Although
o called freehand drawing is deciphered visually, during its preparation, our tactile facilities
y great part, opening the way to the involvement of more than one of our sensory perceptions,
ding the way to establishing the haptic, multi-sensory participation in our environment. Even
e quite limited and limiting definitions of the duties of an architect, as prescribed by the National
uncil of Architectural Registration Boards—to protect the health, safety, and welfare of the cli-
ts—contains the mostly undefined and indefinable term of welfare, which is strongly dependent
m our sensory feedback.

Concerning teaching, first I have to establish my authenticity by sharing some of my (boring)
rsonal history. Authenticity is not so much about authority, but more about being genuine and

trustworthy – sharing my beliefs and how I live and act by them. Next, I share my method, which is free to be borrowed until the student finds her/his own. Lastly, I illustrate that I am loyal to my beliefs and that my method is relevant, since it produced the expected results, even when fulfilling self-proclaimed goal. So the belief + method = relevance equation seems to work as a map for inspiration, and building a need for higher aspirations in the minds and hearts of the students. Sharing goals and achievements and admitting shortcomings or unfulfilled aspirations, one can become a student even in professional practice – as learning is necessary for the whole duration of one's life. The greatest difference between life in the university and life after the university is represented by the different acquisition of knowledge. As we have it at the present time in most of our institutions it is the difference between the predetermined and the undetermined delivery systems. The former is defined by the institutions, mostly for self-serving convenience, since aside from some sequential subjects there seems to be no pedagogical advantage in prescribed grouping or cueing.

Referring earlier to my methods, after close to 100 designs, recorded and boxed, the following sub-processes were observed:

Contents of Operations (CO):
Holder of surface (HS)
Provider of surface (PS)
Geometry of surface (GS)
Mode of Operations (MO):
Data processing (DAP)
Data interpretation (DIP)
Macro-geometrical exploration (MAGEX)
Macro-geometrical articulation (MAGAR)
Micro-geometrical exploration (MIGEX)
Micro-geometrical articulation (MIGAR)

Preliminary presentation (PREP)

Final presentation (PREF)

Source system (SSy):

Every system is composed of subsystems and is at the same time a subsystem of a larger
ga system(s). We have to create a comprehensive source system, which is capable of being the
is of different subsystems. The design simultaneously has to impose limitations (solutions) and
er freedom for the future—as yet unknown—subsystems.

As it has been mentioned, my methods are presented as one possible method, while
dents are encouraged to find their own. I have experienced several times in life that discipline
vides the greatest freedom.

alladian Space-neurons and Other Roots of nfinity

ological Phenomenology of Space-Architecture as Roots of Infinity
er Magyar

Let me start with some disclaimers. I am not a philosopher, and certainly not a phenomenol-
st. In a minute I will explain how this domain came—literally—into the picture. Also, what you
l see is a work in progress dealing mostly with a method of discovery, from which conclusions
ve as yet to be made.

Phenomenology comes from the Greek phainomenon, meaning "that which appears," and
os meaning "study." The first sentence in the thirteen-page-long Wikipedia entry reads as fol-
vs: "(it) is the philosophical study of the structures of experience and consciousness." We will stop

583

there, and I will explain the willful marriage in which I forced topology and phenomenology into. Jean Piaget, the late Swiss philosopher and clinical psychiatrist, after hundreds of actual tests with young children, in his book *The Child's Perception of Space* made the statement that our psyche—consciousness—is organized by topological principles. Also, Maurice Merleau-Ponty, one of the fathers of phenomenology, wrote this in his book *The Primacy of Perception:* "if we are seeking to form an idea of, or to understand the essence of, a spatial figure ... we must first perceive it. Then we will imagine all the aspects contained in the figure as changed. That which cannot be varied without the object itself disappearing is the essence." This is a very important, maybe unintentionally topological, statement. So, goodbye phenomenology, hello topology.

Paul Valery in Eupalinos ou l'Architecte wrote: "Music and Architecture force us, to transcend in thought that which they would seem, in reality, to imply; they rest in the middle of this world like monuments of another world; or like scattered instances of structure and time which are not products of human beings, but of basic forms and laws."

Doing a competition for "A House for Johann Sebastian Bach," I made the following assumption: music can be perceived as a knot on the infinite line of time, while architecture is a spatial-loop (system) on the infinite surface of the Earth, which separates space and non-space. So, the "knotters" and the "loopers" are doing very similar service to humankind: to bring forth, what is un-hearable and in-visible for most everybody, except for those whose existence is rewarded and burdened with this self-imposed duty. Again, knots and loops are very much in the language of topology, so let us see what they mean for our investigation. Topology is the youngest but fast developing and one of the most important aspects of mathematics and geometry. In my studies, this time, I apply only one simplified branch of topology – visual topology. This kind of topological transformation does not conserve the proportions, measurements, or directions, only the continuity and neighborhood relations of the surface are to be un-changed. This could be reffered to as "rubber sheet-geometry," because it deals with that property that an object retains under deformation ially bending, stretching, and squeezing, but not breaking or tearing. Since topology by its re is not scale-specific, topological transformations can be applied from micro to macro scale , industrial design and urban design).

We can then continue with the following assertions: if we free the boundary conditions the measurable (metric) restrictions while applying topological transformations to them, we duce the "Topologically Equivalent Model" and we can call it "general spaceprint" (the essence of erleau-Ponty). Every particular spaceprint is reducible to one general spaceprint, but from one eral spaceprint an unlimited number of particular spaceprints can be generated.

Based on Jean Piaget's research, I forward the hypothesis: there might exist a correlation veen a so called biologically coded formal preference and the similarity of the general and icular spaceprints, which similarity I call topological isomorphy.

According to general practice in architecture, intentionally or unintentionally, the shapes e spaceprints are conceived and articulated by design, and realized through construction. refore, architecture as a design process is the planning of and product of the execution of ropriate changes in the surfaces or spaceprints.

Let us now look at the drawings. On our figures 11 and 12, the upper surface represents stretched, flattened surface of the Earth, including the similarly handled external surfaces of dings. The tubes stand for the openings (windows and doors) connecting the internal surfaces he rooms (in this case the bubbles) with the infinite, or at least immeasurable, Earth face and the erent rooms with each other.

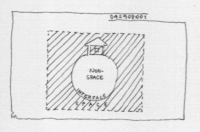

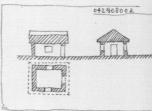

Observations and applications of this method for long years, led to the following simplified, drawn-manifesto:

Figure 01

- Architecture deals with two essential domains: space and non-space.
- Space contains non-space.
- The interface of these domains is named spaceprint (SP), it simultaneously describ
  the localized shapes of both space and non-space.
- The condition of spatial continuity is surface continuity.

Figure 02

- It is common behavior in the practice of architecture that we are talking about spa
  yet non-space is drawn.

586

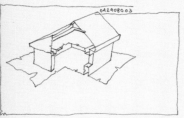 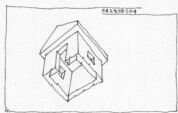

Figures 03 and 04

- Particular spaceprints (PSP) could describe the shapes of an object and as well as of space.
- Intentionally or unintentionally, these spaceprints are imagined in architectural design and materialized in building construction.
- In construction, one distinguishes surface providers and surface holders.
- Traditional materials are bifunctional, while new structures show distinct separation of these two functions.

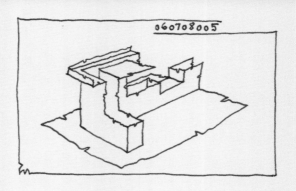

060708005

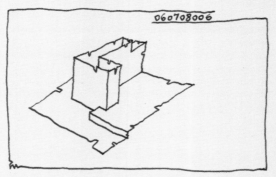

060708006

588

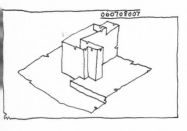 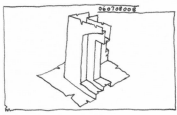

Figures 05, 06, 07, and 08

- Spaceprint fragments (SPF) describe surface strategies; changes in the surface usually denote changes in the structures and/or materials.

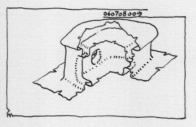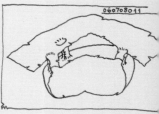

Figures 09 and 10

- Applying to the particular spaceprints the rules of topology, where metric properties (measurements, directions, and proportions) are not preserved, only the neighborhood relationships, we can create the general spaceprints.
- Every particular spaceprint can be transformed to only one general spaceprint, but this latter could be reversed to numberless versions of the former.
- Topological transformations are often called rubber-sheet geometry, hence the rounded shapes and tube-like openings. These latter representing the doors, windows, and other openings, seamlessly connect internal surfaces with the external ones.

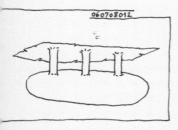 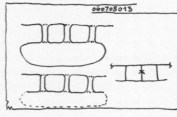

ures 11 and 12

- Applying the infinite pliability of these imaginary surfaces, the general spaceprints (GSP) can be transformed and the result is the simplified general spaceprint (SGSP).

591

This reduction method resulted in a relatively simple tool, which denotes spatial structure, and, as such, could be applied in analytical and comparative studies of space in architecture. As a shorthand depiction, they could be used as a programming tool (in a SGSP format) or in the "bubbles and tubes" version, they can reveal spatial relationships of any building.

These characteristics enable this process, to be applied for the establishment of spatial typologies. These drawings are the intermediary elements through which my investigation method relates to the relationships between architecture, space, and the cosmos.

The visual boundaries—internal or external—allow us to perceive only partial relationships of spatial connectivity. They graciously reduce complexity to visual, easily-digestible sights. Simplicity is still a governing principle for the shaping of individual spaces, or even when the external appearance of a building is concerned. However, under these seemingly simple space perceptions, the incredibly complex spatial structure is hidden, and, so far, the spaceprint method is the only one that is able to reveal the complex system of spatial loops, which are present even in a seemingly simple building.

We can be surprised by the inherent complexity of a seemingly simple building's spatial structures. Seeing this complexity now, it is inevitable to not to see them as root- systems, the root of infinity. This interpretation of architecture reveals omnipresent but newly formulated aspects for the enrichment and ritualization of our spatial perception. With the application of the theoretical tools of reduction and topological transformation, the infinite expansion of space, at least cognitively, can be comprehended. Myriad attempts were made to discover a believable and shared symbolism of architecture since the lost secrets of the Renaissance. The obvious but lost symbol is its cosmic scale. The perception of the presence of gravity and spatial infinity rarely happens. One can easily imagine, that in the case of even one, or many, high-rise buildings, how complex and deep-rooted this connection and symbolic representation of anchoring infinity could become.

We can talk about low-, medium-, high-, super-, and hyper-intensity degrees, and the number mangrove-like roots in the cities (root-fields). Once it is understood that even the simplest uilding has an intimate, and mostly hidden relationship to infinity, architects can become the ew priests and shamans of our society; when they do what their awed predecessors were doing: eaking to and with the cosmos, recording its magnificent presence.

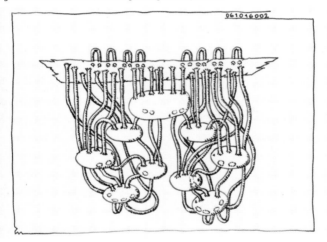

061016002

ttp://en.wikipedia.org/wiki/Phenomenology_(philosophy)
. Piaget (avec B. Inhelder): La représentation de l'espace chez l'enfant. Paris: Presses univ. de France, 1948.
Maurice Merleau-Ponty: Le primat de la perception et ses conséquences philosophiques, in: Bulletin de la Société française de nilosophie, XLI, 1947, p. 119–153.
Paul Valéry: Eupalinos ou L'Architecte, in: Oeuvres de Paul Valéry, vol.2. Paris: Gallimard, 1960.
Peter Magyar: Thought Palaces. Amsterdam: Architectura & Natura Press, 1999.

Biographical Notes
Robert McCarter

Robert McCarter is a practicing architect, professor of architecture, and author. He is the Ruth and Norman Moore Professor of Architecture, and chair of the Architecture Graduate Program at the Sam Fox School of Design and Visual Arts at Washington University in St. Louis. From 1991–200 he was a professor of architecture and for ten years the director of the School of Architecture at the University of Florida. From 1986–1991 he was an associate professor and assistant dean at the Graduate School of Architecture at Columbia University, New York. He has also taught as the Frederic Lindley Morgan Distinguished Professor of Architectural Design at the University of Louisville, has taught at North Carolina State University, and has previously been appointed as a visiting scholar at the American Academy in Rome on three occasions. During his twenty-eight years in academia, including fifteen years in administration, McCarter taught at least one design studio every semeste teaching over 600 students in his career.

McCarter has practiced architecture continuously since he began his internship in 1977 and has been a licensed architect since 1982. From 1991–2007 he was president of D-Mc2 Architecture, P. A., in Tioga, Florida, during which time his firm had twelve buildings constructed to their design. He currently has an architectural practice in St. Louis.

McCarter is the author of *Louis I. Kahn* (Phaidon Press, London, 2005); *On and By Frank Lloyd Wright: A Primer of Architectural Principles* (Phaidon Press, London, 2005); *Frank Lloyd Wright: Critical Lives* (Reaktion Books, London, 2006); *William Morgan: Selected and Current Works* (Images Press, ney, 2002); *Frank Lloyd Wright* (Phaidon Press, London, 1997); *Unity Temple: Frank Lloyd Wright* aidon Press, London, 1997); and *Fallingwater: Frank Lloyd Wright* (Phaidon Press, London, 1994). is currently under contract for *Alvar Aalto: Art & Ideas* (Phaidon Press), *Carlo Scarpa* (Phaidon ss), *Aldo van Eyck* (Yale University Press), and with *Juhani Pallasmaa, Architecture as Experience* aidon Press). He is also currently working on books on a number of contemporary architects as ll as a study of the relationship between painting and architecture from 1900 to today. He edited d contributed essays to several scholarly and professional journals, books, and other publications.

McCarter was selected as one of the "Ten Best Educators" in American schools of architecture he education issue of Architect magazine in December 2009; two books by McCarter, *Louis I. hn* and *On and By Frank Lloyd Wright*, were finalists for the inaugural Royal Institute of British hitects (RIBA) International Book Awards in 2006. McCarter received the Rotch Foundation veling Studio Award in 2003 (one of only ten awarded nationally), with which he took a graduate dio to Finland. In 1989 he received a Graham Foundation Grant in support of his work on Frank yd Wright. He was awarded first prize in the SOM Traveling Fellowship National Design Competi- n in 1983.

Dr. Kendra Schank Smith

Kendra Schank Smith has been the chair of the Department of Architectural Science at Ryerson University since 2007. She holds a Ph.D. in architecture from Georgia Tech where she studied history, theory, and criticism with specialization in representation. She also has a professional degree in architecture (M.Arch) from Virginia Tech. Her primary research explores architectural sketches as part of the thinking process in design, looking at them from memory, imagination, fantasy, caricature, the grotesque, and philosophical theories of play. She has numerous publications on topics of history, theory, and criticism of architecture, media and communication, urbanism, and architectural education, including two books on architectural sketches: *Architect's Drawings: A Selection of Sketches by World Famous Architects Through History* and *Architect's Sketches: Dialogue and Design*. Smith has worked in the office of Kevin Roche John Dinkeloo Associates in Hamden, Connecticut, and has taught at several schools in North America including Texas A&M, the University of Minnesota, and the University of Utah. She teaches design studio and courses in history/theory, representation, and visual communication.

eter Magyar

Dr. Peter Magyar, between 1989 and 2011, served as director of the Schools of Architecture in ree American universities. He holds a Master of Architecture and a Doctor of Architecture degree, th issued by the Technical University of Budapest, Hungary. He was teaching, lecturing, and acticing internationally, and has designed large urban ensembles, some of them are constructed. authored several books about his projects, and in 2011 he won the Pro Architectura Hungarica edal. In 2015 he became a member of the Hungarian (Szecheny) Academy of Arts and Letters. He s elected as a Fellow of the Royal Institute of British Architects in 2016. In 2017 in Berlin, and in 18 in Amsterdam, his drawings and projects respectively were selected as finalists for the World chitecture Festival.

Awknowledgements

My great friends, professor Kendra Schank Smith, Ph.D., and professor Robert McCarter graciously allowed me to reprint their articles that had been previously published in different venues. Since they were addressing my drawings, which have not changed much in the last thirty-some years, their expert comments are still valid now.

To the FAU School of Architecture project I received the drawings of the municipal parking from its designer and my friend, Mr. Donald Singer, FAIA. It was greatly appreciated. (He and his firm were also the designers of the building, which was actually built.)

At the Venice gate project, for the help with the model and the submission drawings, I am very grateful to Daryl Martin, Felicia Davis, Neehlu and Rajesh Yadav.

I would also like to thank my other coauthor, friend, and and wife Celia Gabor, who was present when all the thoughts recorded in these chapters were conceived and executed to different levels of reality. I am immensely grateful and pray for her continuous "presence," as the source of my creative energy.

ooks by Dr. Peter Magyar

Spaceprints, 1986, Auburn University Press.

Construction Meditative, 1988, Auburn Univeristy Press.

Scattered Instances of Structure and Time, 1989, Auburn University Press.

Thought Palaces, 1999, Amsterdam: Architectura & Natura Press.

Thinkink, 2010, Kendall Hunt Publishers.

Urban Innuendoes, 2012, Trafford Publishers.

Seven Lessons on Architectural Morphogenesis, 2013, Trafford Publishers.

The Soft Boiled Egg Scribbles, 2014, K-State University Press.

Bluntly Drawn, 2014, K-State University Press.

Travel Sketches, 2014, Budapest: Kunsthalle.

"Between Bridges," Pen Zen Diaries #1, 2015, Trafford Publishers.

"Consequential Deliberations," Pen Zen Diaries #2, 2015, Trafford Publishers.

"Operation Paris," Pen Zen Diaries #3, 2015, Trafford Publishers.

"Angles and Oranges," Pen Zen Diaries #4, 2015, Trafford Publishers.

"Multiple Horizons," Pen Zen Diaries #5, 2015, Trafford Publishers.

"Hesitant Decisions," Pen Zen Diaries #6, 2015, Trafford Publishers.

Making Evergreen Architecture, W. A. Lazar, 2016, LitFire Publishing.

Palladian Space-neurons, 2016, LitFire Publishing.

Pen Zen Diaries (# 1 and 2) 2018, Trafford Publishers.

ORO Editions
Publishers of Architecture, Art, and Design
Gordon Goff: Publisher

www.oroeditions.com
info@oroeditions.com

Published by ORO Editions

Text by Peter Magyar
Foreword by György Szegő
With essays by Robert McCarter and Kendra Schank Smith
Book Design by Brooke Biro
Managing Editor: Jake Anderson
10 9 8 7 6 5 4 3 2 1 First Edition
ISBN: 978-1-943532-15-5
Color Separations and Printing: ORO Group Ltd.
Printed in China.